# I WAS A PEER SUPPORT SPECIALIST

# *I WAS A PEER SUPPORT SPECIALIST*

*John Friday*

I was a Peer Support Specialist
Copyright © 2018 by John D. Friday
All rights reserved. No portion of this book may be reproduced, stored in a retrieval system, or transmitted in any form or by any means (electronic,
mechanical, photocopy, recording, scanning, or other) except for brief quotations
in critical reviews or articles, without the prior written permission of the publisher.

Independently Published
Printed in the United States of America

This book is dedicated with gratitude to my Lord Jesus,
who blessed me and guided me throughout my
vocation and recovery journey as a peer support specialist.

I thank my wife Jackie, my mentor Ken, and my friends for their
encouragement and support in writing this text of my journey as a
peer support specialist.

# CONTENTS

1 THE JOURNEY BEGINS .................................................................................... 1
2 THE SALVATION ARMY ................................................................................... 9
3 SAFE HARBOR PEER SERVICES ................................................................. 15
4 FRIENDSHIP PROGRAM ............................................................................... 22
5 BANNER YEARS ............................................................................................... 29
6 SEASONED VOCATION .................................................................................. 35
7 MENTAL HEALTHCARE ................................................................................ 41
8 THE NEBRASKA FACTOR ............................................................................. 48
9 THE V.A. FACTOR ........................................................................................... 56
10 MY MENTAL HEALTH .................................................................................. 61
11 ADDITIONAL SUPPORTS ........................................................................... 66
12 ARTWORK AND MY MENTAL ILLNESS ................................................. 71
BIBLIOGRAPHY AND RECOMMENDED READINGS ................................ 85

# 1 THE JOURNEY BEGINS

*God is gracious.*

I was a peer support specialist. At first glance, one might say that my journey began in September of 2010, when I was hired by The Salvation Army for their Emergency Community Support Services program as a part-time peer support specialist.

I had held many jobs over the course of my life, but this would turn out to be more than a career. It was a vocation for which I developed a great passion. To qualify for the position, I had to have lived experience of personal mental illness, and/or trauma, and/or substance abuse. Hence, the "peer" aspect of the peer support specialist. I served individuals who struggled with mental illness and/or trauma issues, like myself. Through God's grace, I had been prepared over the years for this vocation from virtually the time I was born. And, from the realization of that vocation grew my passion.

Initially, I knew nothing about peer support. I had a job coach who was certain that, with my background, I would be well matched to this position. I applied for this job, unaware of how I would do it. Soon after applying I had a telephone interview. It lasted over thirty minutes. I was invited to a second interview in the hiring manager's office the next day. Two managers were sitting across from me, and it lasted about an hour. During the interview I shared my journey of mental illness and trauma. To me it was just the path that my life had taken. At the interview's conclusion, the primary manager told me that I would be a natural at this job. They offered it to me, and I accepted.

Even so, I was still unsure as to what I would be doing. The manager was also my supervisor and took me under her wing. She loaned me a training manual on intentional peer support. I did more than read it; I drank it in. I was grasping for some understanding of what peer support was, and how I was supposed to be doing it.

There were two other part-time peer support specialists who had been in peer support for a while longer than me. One worked during the day; the other worked in the afternoon and early evening. We had set days to work, but flexible hours. That was so that we could adjust our hours to meet with our peers at their convenience. Many had to meet with other service agencies that had set hours of operation, so that they could try to get assistance; some with housing vouchers, or financial assistance, or food stamps, etc. As noted above, we were an emergency community support services program. Our social workers helped our peers get the community support that they needed.

I learned that peer support specialists were a relatively new phenomenon in the state of Nebraska, although peer support had been practiced in the mental health communities of many other states.

As stated above, having lived experience of mental illness and/or substance abuse was a key requirement of the job. Another was to have completed a workshop on the Wellness Recovery Action Plan (WRAP). This was a way of managing one's mental health symptoms and behaviors developed by Mary Ellen Copeland, Ph.D. (1997). I had taken the workshop the weekend prior to applying for the job, at the urging of my job coach.

In the workshop I learned the key concepts of WRAP, and, with the facilitator's guidance, I learned how to develop a WRAP for myself. Initially, my personal plan was very crude. Nonetheless, I made efforts to use the plan as it was intended by Dr. Copeland. I have learned over the years, as Dr. Copeland observed about herself in one of her videos, that, like her, my repertoire of wellness strategies grew over time. One or two coping skills were not enough to weather the storms of mental illness. To learn more about WRAP see Dr. Copeland's website: www.copelandcenter.com.

The other two peer support specialists were great resources of the art of peer support. They were not able to take me on their appointments, but they were always willing to sit down between appointments and share their knowledge and expertise in their roles as peer support specialists.

The lady peer support specialist invited me to observe her as she called and made appointments with new peers that had been referred to her by the department's case managers. During the case managers' intake process, they ask their clients if they would be interested in meeting with a peer support specialist, either in the specialist's office, or, if needed, in the peer's home. Because of difficulties with transportation, most chose to meet with a peer support specialist in their home.

I determined that the only way I was going to learn about peer support at that time was by doing it. I talked with the two peer support specialists about their experiences. Within a few weeks I was assigned a peer to work with in the office.

# I WAS A PEER SUPPORT SPECIALIST

My efforts were at first very clumsy. Most of what I did was ask open ended questions, just as one would do with any new acquaintance. We got to know each other. I shared some of my story with them, as it related to what they were sharing. This was not to one up their experience, but to let them know that they were not alone in their mental health struggles.

Soon I took steps to call other peers that had been referred to us for peer support. I began to have a case load of peers that I visited in their homes. I always felt that I should be doing more, so I began to share what I knew about WRAP, helping them to develop Wellness Recovery Action Plans of their own. That gave me a little more to do as I met with them.

In January 2011, Nebraska initiated a training program that would prepare individuals to take a peer support and wellness specialist examination. I applied for and was accepted to take the 40-hour week long training course developed by Shery Mead, in conjunction with Yale University. A group of pioneers had taken the first course, and in turn became the facilitators of our course.

I learned about the four tasks of this model of intentional peer support: connection, worldview, mutuality, and moving toward. We studied a brief history of peer support and mental illness. We also studied active listening skills. We practiced a lot of role playing situations. We studied the peer support code of ethics. In addition, we were separated into groups of four or five, and given the assignment of working together to demonstrate our understanding of the four tasks, and any other aspect of the study material that we wanted to include. All the groups did excellent.

One can learn more about this model by visiting Shery Mead's website: www.intentionalpeersupport.org.

Once I completed the course, I looked for ways to implement what I had learned. The following month I took the state test for certification. The written portion took most of the morning for me to complete. In the afternoon, I took the oral portion before a panel of three examiners. It was weeks before I learned that I had passed. I was then awarded the title of Certified Peer Support and Wellness Specialist (CPSWS).

It was affirming to know that I had grasped the material I had studied. Now, it was an issue of moving from knowledge of the material to internalizing the peer support model as a guide to my serving my fellow peers. That would take time and practice. In any case, I was proud of my achievement.

Our training did not end with being certified. There were continuing education courses that had to be taken on a yearly basis. Most of those courses were taken through workshops offered at the annual Nebraska DHHS behavioral healthcare conference. I greatly enjoyed the workshops and keynote speakers. I learned more about skills peer support specialists across the state were using. I learned about trauma informed care, compassion fatigue, ways to nurture our own mental health, etc... There were vendors of different mental healthcare companies that shared products, and books that were available to help us increase our skills as peer support specialists. It was an awesome experience. But that was not all our continuing education. There were in-service courses that The Salvation Army had us attend, as well. They covered all sorts of topics relevant to working as a mental health provider.

About a year after my certification as a peer support specialist, I attended another week-long training course; this time to become a Wellness Recovery Action Plan (WRAP) facilitator. This provided me with the formal skills and knowledge to instruct others in the ways of the WRAP. I was still new to peer support, and I stumbled in many ways, but, I did not stop trying to meet the needs of those I served. It was in the relationships that developed between the peers and me that I learned the meaning of peer support.

Some of the peers, once we met for the first time, and they learned a little bit more about peer support, declined peer support services. And, that was alright. Peer support is strictly voluntary. A peer cannot be forced to engage in peer support. Most of the individuals referred to us, though, participated in the services.

Instead of focusing on the WRAP, however, I began to actively listen to the peers, as he or she shared some of their stories. We frequently developed the trust between us that was needed to connect and share some of our most painful and frustrating experiences. From time to time a peer would tell me that the things they shared with me they had not shared with their doctor, or with family members. The experiences were that painful. And, the peers thought that these individuals would not understand. Some had experienced stigma even within their circle of family and friends. Peers noted that it meant a great deal to them to have the opportunity to share those experiences with someone who had experienced similar mental health struggles.

There was a foundational element to the trust we built between us. That was confidentiality. As I noted to them, I would not divulge what they shared with me. The exception was if I got the impression that they were going to hurt themselves, or someone else. As I explained, by law I had to report that to my supervisor, and possibly report it to a 911 operator.

But, even I, with my own mental illness, had occasional nuisance thoughts of self-harm. These were not thoughts I entertained with any seriousness or urge to carry out. They were a product of the chemical imbalance on my brain. Or, so I have been told. If I trusted my mental health provider, I shared these thoughts with them. My hesitancy was dependent on whether I felt sharing with the wrong person might result in my being hospitalized when I felt that it was not yet necessary.

# I WAS A PEER SUPPORT SPECIALIST

My primary reason for sharing with my mental health provider was to get an idea of the nature of my mental illness, and for determining whether I needed an adjustment to my medication, especially if the thoughts were becoming more frequent. It was in my best interest to share the thoughts with those who might be able to assist me with managing my mental health.

Just because, at the time, I had not been in the hospital for several years, did not mean that I did not have my own mental health struggles. I used my WRAP, just as I encouraged others to do. I had my favorite coping strategies. I found over time that I usually needed a collection of strategies to ride the storm of mental illness.

Occasionally, while a peer was sharing some of what they were feeling, they would occasionally share some of the nuisance thoughts of their own. We would discuss them in more depth and explore whether they had a plan to carry out these thoughts. Sometimes they did have the intention to implement their plan, and I acted accordingly. Usually, they did not, and they assured me of that fact. I trusted our relationship enough to accept their word. We would also explore whether they had the means to carry out their thoughts of self-harm. If I was concerned about what they were sharing, I let them know. I also let them know that I was going to share what they told me with my supervisor. Sometimes the peer got angry. But, I had rather they get angry with me, and be alive, than the alternative.

On those few occasions, they forgave me. One later thanked me, telling me that I had saved their life. This approach came from my own experiences of wanting to seriously harm myself. In looking back, this desire and urge I had was a result of a deeper longing I had to escape the tremendous emotional pain that I was experiencing at the time.

On one occasion, as I struggled with the thoughts and anguish of having lost my five years old son to divorce, I was driving down a multiple lane highway in Houston, Texas. There were three eighteen-wheelers side by side coming up behind me. The urge to flip the steering wheel of my little Toyota Tercel in front of them was overwhelming. All I could do was repeatedly scream at the top of my lungs the words "NO!! NO!! NO!!" until I reached the Veteran's Affairs (VA) Hospital. The emergency room gave me a bottle of antidepressants and referred me to the Vet Center across town for outpatient therapy. It got me through the storm. There were other occasions. Some involved the police, some did not.

I will note here that the police were always very compassionate with the way they handled my crisis situations. Once I tried to explain to the officers that it was okay for me to take my life. I noted that I was going to use pills, and just drift into oblivion, as I listened to my favorite new age music by Enya. They kindly responded that they could not let me do that; then gently putting me in handcuffs and got me the help that I needed.

John Friday

Not all my efforts with peers ended with positive healthy results. I remember one peer that completed suicide. She told me of her intention. We talked about it. She was very angry when I told her that I was going to have to share her situation with my supervisor. Which is what I did.

My supervisor and I talked it over as soon as I got back to the office. The sticking point was that I did not see that she had the means to complete the suicide plan. I was wrong. She did find a way. She had told me that, if I did call the police, when they showed up she would tell them that she was doing okay and not intending to harm herself. She would lie. She told me that they would not be able to do anything. She knew the system well and how to play it.

I remember her often, especially on the anniversary of her death. I see her face and wonder what I could have said that would have changed her mind and saved her life. As a result, I became a lot more willing to call 911 than perhaps I had been before. I became a lot more willing to accept the peer's anger with me, even if it meant that they might never talk to me ever again.

On another occasion, I arrived at the home of a peer for a scheduled appointment. This was the first time I had met with them. They gave me a tour of their dwelling. Then I was escorted into the kitchen, where I sat down at their dinette table. The peer paced around the room as they shared some of their story. The more they paced the room, the more agitated and louder they became. I was feeling more and more uncomfortable with the situation and began wondering about my safety. I was being triggered by the situation. It was more than I could bare. I needed to leave and began looking for the way out. I interrupted the peer's telling of their story, and politely noted that I had to leave and would call them when I got back to the office. Which is what I did. Once out of the situation, I was able to use some of the coping strategies I had from my WRAP. That helped a lot.

I called the peer and explained that I had been triggered by the situation. That was the reason I had to leave. We discussed the experience. I noted that I was willing to meet with them in my office, but that I did not feel comfortable meeting in their home. Unfortunately, the peer was not willing to meet me in my office. That ended our sessions. I discussed the situation and outcome with my supervisor, who understood my position. If I do not feel safe in a session, I am not going to be of much good to my peer. There is a need for mutuality. We both need to feel comfortable that we are in a safe environment.

With each of my peers, I tried to understand their worldview. I focused on them, and what they were sharing. While they were talking, I let go of the temptation to think of how I was going to respond. We sat with each other, caught in the moment. What were they sharing? What was their body language? In time, I stopped worrying about my own body language, as I leaned forward, and hung onto each thought and feeling they communicated. I asked questions to clarify to myself that I understood what they shared. I often repeated back to them what they had said, only in the way that I understood it. Sometimes, they would correct my grasp of their thoughts. Or, they would nod their heads, and continue with their story. We took mutual responsibility for our part in understanding each other. At the time, that was how I understood the need for mutuality in our peer-to-peer relationship.

The fourth task in Shery Mead's model of peer support is "working toward". I struggled in my initial understanding of this task. I saw it as meaning a goal, a destination. How could I, as a peer support specialist, help my peer to identify and attain a goal of peer support? The added problem was that the services of The Salvation Army Emergency Community Support Service program lasted for only a three-month period. In some cases, a one-month extension was given on top of that. So, at most, I might be able to work with a peer for about six months. We only met once a week, for about an hour. It seemed like such a short time in the lived experience. Often, peers would say that they wished that they had longer access to peer support; they had experienced such benefit from it. Unfortunately, I could not locate another agency in my area of Nebraska that provided peer support services without the peer having to join a day group program of some sort.

The people with whom I served are some of the bravest people I know. One mother had gotten involved with hard core street drugs. Many in her circle of friends were addicted to street drugs. She noted that her best friend was a drug dealer. One of the consequences of her lifestyle, however, was that her children had been taken away from her, and she lost her custodial rights. She missed her children tremendously.

This mother decided that what she wanted to work toward was regaining her custodial rights to her children. We discussed what would be the path toward that goal. One of the things she noted that she needed to do was change her circle of friends. We talked about the kinds of friends that would be supportive of her new lifestyle. Then she and I talked about where one would find such supporters. She concluded that she could develop those new relationships at a church of her choice. She severed all ties with her old friends, especially her one-time best friend. The mother recognized that her best friend was no best friend, if that person pulled her back into a drug abusing culture.

The mother took steps to attend a church of her choice and talk with the pastor and his wife. She shared some of her story with them. They welcomed her into the church, a first step in developing the circle of friends that would be supportive of the lifestyle she had begun seeking.

The course of life's journey is not always an easy one. We talked about an occasion in which she briefly lapsed. She and I agreed that the journey has high points and low points. A stumble is not the end of the journey. What is important is that she does not give up, and that she has the courage to get up and continue the

## John Friday

journey toward what is important to her. In this case, it was regaining custody of her children.

The last time I saw that determined mother, she was still working toward the life that she wanted. I have seen the same of other peers I served for The Salvation Army. Some wanted new housing. Others wanted a job. Some, like this young mother, wanted to be reunited with their children. All wanted a better life for themselves and their families.

God is gracious.

\* \* \*

## 2 THE SALVATION ARMY

*God is gracious.*

It was in the relationships that developed between the peers and me that I learned the meaning of peer support. While serving the peers of The Salvation Army, I was invited into their homes in hope that something good would come of it.

Those first couple of years of being a peer support specialist were clumsy, and uncertain. I did not understand how developing a relationship served any good. I kept thinking that I needed to be doing something. I remember sitting in people's homes thinking that the only thing I had to offer was how to develop a Wellness Recovery Action Plan (WRAP). But, not everyone was interested in developing a WRAP. Some had created one in other agencies' programs but did not use them.

But, people kept inviting me to return. We usually spent about an hour together. Sometimes we talked about what was bothering them. Sometimes there were issues with family, such as their teenage or adult children. It is interesting that, as down and out as some of the peers were, their major concern was their family.

I tended to feel helpless to do anything for them. I focused on my desire to assist them, instead of just being present to them and listening. I did not yet understand that what I was doing was important to them. Some were losing their homes, and they were scared. It seemed to help to have someone listen who understood. And, I did understand. I remember being one step away from living on the streets, when my ex-wife and her husband stepped in and invited me to live in their basement until I could get back on my feet. They said that they were not going to sit by and let the father of our son end up on the streets while they had room in their home with which to take me in. It was God sent. It lasted a year, but I was able to get back on my feet, and eventually move into an apartment of my own.

As a peer support specialist for The Salvation Army I sometimes drove 40 or 50 miles to just be with a peer, and listen to their concerns, their fears, their hopes, their dreams. As I noted above, I sometimes shared some of my own experiences;

when it related to what they were sharing. I think that the next thing to my listening to them, was the fact that I cared. Sometimes I shared my perspective of how I saw things. Sometimes I could just encourage them to continue the struggle. Sometimes I commended them on how far they had come. Sometimes, after having driven so far, I would get there, and the peer would be high from sniffing nail polish or having taken some street drug. But, still I listened.

Sometimes I travelled so far only to learn that the peer was not there. But, what was important was that I was there. It was important to me that I reached out in whatever way I could.

Some lived in nice homes or apartments. Some lived in one room dives downtown. Like I had noted above, some lived in their ex-spouse's basement. Some had partners living with them; some did not. Some were hoping to get back together with their spouse. Some were hoping to get back together with their children. Like myself, some lamented the direction their teenage or adult children had taken. We were not that different. We were peers.

Some of my peers did not want to take the medication that their doctors prescribed for them. They did not like the way it made them feel. Even so, I encouraged them to continue to take their medication. I noted how I took my medication, sometimes for no other reason than the fact that the alternative behavior for me was unacceptable. I shared how my medication and therapy were helping me. I would like to say that made a difference and they went back to taking their medication. But, often it did not change things. At least I gave them something to think about.

It is interesting to be with someone who is at the bottom and has no way to go but up. All were trying to be creative, as they struggled to make ends meet. There was courage there. It helped me see my own courage in my own struggles. It made me want to be there for them in whatever way I could, so I actively listened. And, I listened with empathy and concern.

I wanted to be there for them. Whether only a few blocks away, or an hour's drive, I kept going out to be with them. It was not just a job. These peers were people. I saw them sometimes down, but not broken. Watching them. Being there with them gave me courage. They were brave souls. Heroes in my book.

There were some peers that had deep demons haunting them. Some let me in. They were in a lot of pain, frequently related to strong relationships, such as family. They had a secret; an intense desire to harm themselves.

Often there was a lot of anger wrapped in that anguish. Even after I told them that, if I thought they were going to harm themselves, by law I had to tell my supervisor, and possibly call a 911 operator. It did not seem to matter. They were willing to talk to me anyway. I think that they wanted to be heard, especially by someone who would understand their experience, their hurt.

# I WAS A PEER SUPPORT SPECIALIST

It is difficult to negotiate life with someone when they do not want to hear it. I can understand, from my own lived experience, why one would want to harm one's self as a means of escaping the anguish that they are experiencing. I, too, have been driven to seeking self-harm as a means of escape. Fortunately, others stepped in and changed the course of my actions. I lived to see the day when my life was thriving, and happy. But, that took time. It did not happen instantly.

When someone is in that place of pain and hopelessness, self-harm seems to make all the sense in the world. I rationalized away all the previous reasons for staying alive: "I was created for Hell!" "I advised my ex-wife that, if something happened to me, she was to tell my young son that I had been killed in an automobile accident." It seemed a fitting excuse. In my mind, this cleared the way for me to complete suicide.

I was not thinking of anyone else. I was focused only on escaping the torturous agony of life, and the hopeless situation in which I had found myself. I felt that I could not go on any longer. Taking my life seemed like a rational and desirable end to the problem. The peers that have shared their own struggles with life and with death seemed to share in this perspective...this way of viewing the world, at least, at that time.

But, with the help of others, I worked through the problem of suicide, and life. I am still alive. More importantly I am enjoying the life I have.

How do I explain that to someone who is in the anguish that I once experienced? They did not want to hear of an alternative that was different from their own. It was fine that things turned out fine for me, but they saw themselves as too damned for anything happy befalling them. They are not open to a solution other than their own demise. They told me that they had tried everything else, and nothing helped.

Again, I listened with compassion. And, I was puzzled as to what another solution would be. I cannot decide the course of their life. It was not up to me to find the solution. It was up to them to find the next best solution that best fit them. It is up to them to weather the storm of mental illness, and life's struggles. I can encourage, but I cannot live it for them. I can share my journey in hopes that they find something redeeming in it.

The problem I encountered was that they may not be open to any other solution at the time, because they are not thinking rationally, only emotionally. The pain is real, and they feel it intensely. They have lost hope of escape by any other means.

I found myself questioning myself. How can I find hope for them again? I listen with support. And, I share with them my own experience of pain and hopelessness. I share my experience of pushing further down the road of life with the help of others, and finding a life worth living, worth enjoying... a life that thrives, and not just exists. But, often it is beyond belief for them. It makes me feel so helpless.

My temptation is to try to take on the task of finding a solution that they can live with. But, only they can find that solution. The reality for me is that helping them find the solution is outside my skill set. I am a listener. I can listen with concern and compassion. I can validate their experiences. I can share my lived experience of weathering the storm in the hope of better days. I can get them the professional help of people far more qualified than myself.

It is sometimes a hard thing, calling the 911 operator, even for the good of the peer. It is something that I do not take lightly, and I confer with my supervisor before taking that kind of action. Frequently, it is the supervisor who takes over and makes the call for a wellness check by the police.

Sometimes the peer gets extremely angry, and vows never to talk to me again. Some try to put guilt trips on me, saying that they trusted me, and that I had betrayed that trust. The thing is, I would rather they be so angry as to never talk to me again, than they be dead. But, not all stay angry. Some understand and forgive. Some are even appreciative.

A frustrating part of this situation is that some peers are so determined to die that they never give up until they succeed. As noted earlier, even if we call 911, and the police are called out, the police can only do so much. If the peer meets the police at the door of their home, and tells the police that they are fine, and are not going to harm themselves, the police can only note it and leave. Then, in solitude, the peer can take their own life. That leaves me wondering what I could have said that would have made a difference to them. What would have motivated them to seek life?

I also sometimes served people who had suffered great traumas. Often, I did not know this until they had begun to share about these traumas. Sometimes the trauma was rape, domestic violence, or some other form of abuse, whether as a child or an adult. I identified with their experience. I, too, had been traumatized as a child of domestic violence, molestation, sexual harassment, and more. Even so, their sharing did not trigger me. Instead, I felt that I was not alone.

On occasions, when the peer was a lady who had experienced sexual assault, I would ask if they would prefer to work with a female peer support specialist. Sometimes they did. And, that was okay.

In serving the peer, I just actively listened as they shared some of their story. I asked clarifying questions to ensure that I understood their story. Out of respect, I did not probe. Rather, I let them share at their own pace whatever they wanted to share. I did not pressure them to share on any given topic. I remained sensitive to the fact that this was hard for them to share. But, at the same time giving them an opportunity to be heard and validated in their experience. At times, I shared some of my own story, as it related to what they were sharing. I did so without getting into the gory details.

Sometimes peers would have relapses, and I would visit them in the hospital. I would listen to their stories of what had happened that resulted in their being hospitalized. Such visits helped to strengthen our relationships.

When I was first a peer support specialist, I was not too concerned about safety. But, I learned that it was an issue. Or, that it could become an issue quickly. Of the two years that I was with The Salvation Army, only once did I become concerned about my safety. Fortunately, I was not shy about getting out of a situation when I was triggered. I learned to be aware of my surroundings, as well as not letting a peer come between me and the nearest exit. This was true even for my office visits. I also learned to encourage the peer to sit with me, rather than pace around the room. I also attended and participated in in-service workshops that covered issues of personal safety, and deescalating volatile situations.

I owe The Salvation Army a lot in giving me my start in peer support. I enjoyed serving the peers that were the clients of The Salvation Army.

God is gracious.

* * *

John Friday

# 3 SAFE HARBOR PEER SERVICES

*God is gracious.*

I served the peers of The Salvation Army as a part-time peer support specialist for about two years. Then I had the opportunity to pursue a full-time peer support specialist position with Community Alliance's Safe Harbor Peer Services program. My understanding was that, at that time, it was intended to be one of only a few peer-run and peer managed warm lines and crisis diversion centers in the world. There were other warm lines, but not usually staffed or run by peers. As far as I was told there were none like it in Nebraska. It would be open twenty-four hours a day, seven days per week.

I, along with the new staff, started training in July 2012. It lasted about a month. The instruction we took was in the form of lecture, discussion, and role play. We trained eight hours a day, five days per week. We studied warm lines, crisis situations, deescalating crisis situations, different types of telephone calls, and more.

The warm line is a telephone help line, but it is a step down from a hotline, such as 911. The idea was to give peers the ability to talk things out prior to the situation becoming a crisis that leads to hospitalization. We would listen and try to deescalate intensely emotional situations. If appropriate, we were able to invite the peer to visit the Safe Harbor crisis diversion center to meet face-to-face with a trained and certified peer support and wellness specialist. If necessary, and the peer reached a crisis level over the phone, we would call the 911 operator, and transfer the call to them. For those who were in the center, when needed, we walked them over to the on premises behavioral healthcare hospital for evaluation and urgent care.

Once we had completed training, we had an open house. A lot of people, including special guests, attended. Each of the staff were spread throughout the center to explain the different areas available to our peer guests.

The warm line center was in a room of its own in Safe Harbor. As for the Safe Harbor center itself, there was a sitting room when one first entered. There were two relaxation rooms that allowed peers to rest, if they were feeling anxious and needed some alone space. There was a community room with a couch, arm chairs, and several tables. There was a kitchenette where we had snacks for the peer guests. Peers could bring food from home to eat, or medication that they needed to take during their stay. We had a sound system for piped in music. There was a wall-mounted television, though we never used it.

There was a wall lined with book shelves, from the floor to virtually the ceiling. That was where the library was meant to be. At the open house, the wall was bare of reading material. I overheard the manager speaking with a visitor, noting that he was hoping that a benefactor would step forward, and fund the library. That did not happen.

I do not know why, but I got it into my head that I would adopt the library. After the open house, I went out and bought $350.00 worth of books for the library. I purchased a variety of texts, workbooks, and novels, all dealing in some way with mental illness, or substance abuse. I had even acquired the Alcoholics Anonymous "Big Book".

I was able to order free literature online from the "National Institute on Mental Health" (NIMH), "Substance Abuse and Mental Health Services Administration" (SAMHSA). I also got brochures from the "National Alliance on Mental Illness" (NAMI). It was not long before I had the library fully stocked.

Peer guests were able to take literature with them during and at the end of their visit at Safe Harbor. The manager was very appreciative of my contribution, and hard work, and allowed me to continue as the unofficial librarian.

The powers that be decided not to advertise about Safe Harbor. Instead, they were going to rely on the news of Safe Harbor to spread by word of mouth. They expected a flood of peers to swamp Safe Harbor, as soon as word got out. We did visit a few non-profit agencies, and made presentations informing their participants about Safe Harbor. Even so, visits and calls turned out to be very slow in manifesting themselves those first few months.

We eventually started getting calls from various parts of Nebraska. We also heard from peers in Iowa. As peer support specialists we actively listened to and validated them as they shared some of their story. Some were just lonely souls wanting to talk. Calls usually lasted from thirty minutes to an hour. Some were longer, as needed.

We were required to maintain records of our calls. For several of us, this was something of an issue. In peer support, our conversations were confidential, yet we were being asked to keep records of those conversations. Management noted that, for them, it was a billing issue. At the same time, the information gathered documented that the program was needed and being used by the community. We were not given a choice. They paid our salaries.

But, there was some leeway. Peers could call in as anonymous callers. We were still required to ask for their name, but we did not push it. In addition, there was a structure to what information the summary of the conversation could take. I documented why they were calling. For example, "The peer was having some family issues." What did I, as a peer support specialist, do? "I actively listened to, and validated the peer, as they shared some of their story. I shared some of my story, as it related to what the peer shared." Finally, what was the outcome? "The peer thanked me and said that they were feeling much better." I satisfied the need for documentation, and at the same time remained true to the need for confidentiality.

Visiting the center was handled a bit differently. I recorded their full name. They could not be anonymous and receive services in the center. There was some demographic and emergency contact information that was also collected. In addition, the visiting peer had to sign a "Consent to Treat" form before services would be provided. Again, I summarized what took place during the peer's visit. What brought them to the center? What did I do? (peer support, conversation, art journaling, WRAP, etc.) And, what was the outcome? Like the warm line calls, this information was logged into a secured computer system, overseen by the IT manager.

Unlike the Salvation Army, Safe Harbor peer support specialists had shift change. Part of the team would cover the phones, while a selected member brought the relieving team up to speed on any issues that had been encountered during the previous shift. The focus was on any peer visitors that might be in the center. Why were they here? What had been done so far, and what suggestions might be considered, regarding what still needed to be done.

When the center first became operational, we had a lot of time on our hands, so we talked amongst ourselves. One lady with whom I worked shared about her art journal. She noted that it was a witness to her life's journey. In her own spare time, she was studying art journaling online. Eventually, she was able to introduce it as an activity shared in the Safe Harbor center. It gave people the opportunity to express with art what they were experiencing.

Art Journaling is a lot like a regular journal, except one uses a picture to communicate the feelings and thoughts one is having on the topic being journaled. There are no rules to art journaling. Some like to use a collage approach to their journaling, using clippings from old magazines, books, calendars, etc... They glue the images that best express what they are experiencing into their art journal.

Much later, with my friend's guidance in the technical aspects of art journaling, I, too, was able to start art journaling. But, for me, at the time, it was a private tool that I added to my own Wellness Recovery Action Plan (WRAP). In time, I would take some of my art journal entries and convert them into watercolor paintings that I displayed in art exhibits. It was an honor to share my journey in that way.

In the center, I still worked with interested peer guests, facilitating the development of their own WRAP. We would discuss activities that they liked to do when they were well to be used to weather the storm of mental illness when they find themselves being triggered, as well as other situations outlined by Dr. Mary Ellen Copeland in her WRAP literature. No one was forced to develop a WRAP. It was strictly voluntary. And, some said thank you, but passed on the opportunity. They just wanted to talk. And so, I listened.

Rarely, but sometimes when a peer came into Safe Harbor, they were found to have been drinking alcohol, and in no condition to take advantage of the peer services the center offered. When I came across that situation, I would talk to the individual in private, and point out that they really were not in a condition where we could help them. We were not a detox facility. We could refer them, if they wanted. And, I noted that, once they were sober, I would be happy to bring them into the center to receive services. But, at that time, they were going to have to leave. I never had any trouble with them. They seemed to respect our position and left. I do not remember if any ever came back. I know that we did have repeat peer visitors, though.

Everyone on the team was very supportive of each other. Sometimes I would get a difficult call. But, after such a call, my co-workers encouraged me to take a break while they covered the phones, which I did. And, I did the same for them. Working there was very much like being with family.

So, what would qualify as a difficult call? Difficult calls might be some peer who is having thoughts of harming themselves. They do not want to call the 911 operator. One does not want to push too hard, or the caller might hang up. One works the call, trying to get the phone number of where the peer is. The caller is having a difficult time weathering the storm of their situation. Such a call might last over an hour. And, eventually, they might either agree to come into the Safe Harbor center or go to the emergency room at the hospital.

Often, peers were hesitant about calling the 911 operator, because the operator got the police involved. Peers did not want to be handcuffed in front of their neighbors, family, or friends. They found it humiliating. It was a very emotional issue to many callers. Peers tended to be more willing to come into the center, or go to the emergency room, if they could drive themselves.

On one occasion, I was on the phone listening and speaking with a peer bent on self-harm for six hours. At the end we had reached a stalemate. He did agree to call back again, though. That was something. We took it a day at a time. Eventually, he stopped calling, and I never heard from him again. I do not know what happened to him.

One drawback to the Safe Harbor center was that we did not have the ability to provide transportation to bring peers into the center. And, frequently callers did not have transportation to reach Safe Harbor. However, sometimes family or friends were able to bring the caller into the center for help.

Our manager was also a peer support specialist and had his office in Safe Harbor center. Once a week we individually met with him in what was called a Co-Supervision meeting. I would talk about what was going on with me and the interactions that I had on the phones and in the center. For me, I needed some feedback on how I was doing. I also felt a need to be validated.

My manager was in that first group of peer support specialists trained directly by Shery Mead, the principal agent in helping to put together the peer support and wellness specialist curriculum used by the state of Nebraska to train and certify peer support specialists. I looked a lot to my manager for guidance in perfecting my skills as a peer support specialist. I learned a great deal from him. It was called Co-Supervision, because he sought input in ways, as our manager, he could be of service to us. Fact was, though, because he was also a peer support specialist, he understood where we were coming from and was very helpful in guiding and supporting us.

In addition, we had our team meetings on Saturday mornings from ten o'clock to noon in Safe Harbor's community room. Everyone from all the shifts was required to attend. Snacks and coffee were provided. The manager would discuss any issues needing to be addressed to the team. Sometimes someone would have to step out of the meeting to answer the warm line. That person was brought up to speed later.

One year I had a choice of conferences to attend, either the annual behavioral healthcare conference, or the first annual conference just for peer support specialists. I chose to go to the Peer Support Specialists Conference. Like the behavioral healthcare conference, the peer support conference was going to have workshops for continuing education credits. But there was an added element to this conference. It was going to address the issue of making Nebraska peer support services Medicaid billable.

It was a hot issue. Some peer support specialists were hesitant about supporting it, because other states had experienced Medicaid dictating the terms of how and for how long a peer could receive services from a peer support specialist. Some specialist felt that we were able to do more for peers without Medicaid's interference. Other peer support specialists felt that the adjustments were worth the opportunity to obtain more funding for peer support services. It was thought that more agencies would be able to afford to hire more peer support specialists. That would open peer support for a lot of peers who could not otherwise afford it. It made for an interesting dialogue at the conference. As for me, I tended to support making peer support Medicaid billable.

On another note, I had the opportunity to help with the week-long training of police officers to join the Crisis Intervention Team (CIT). The Crisis Intervention Teams were made up of specially trained police officers who were called out to respond to crisis situations involving people with mental illnesses. These police officers volunteered for this duty. A peer support specialist was also assigned to the team.

Various peers were recruited to help with this training. It gave officers the occasion to hear from those who have mental illness issues in a different setting.

I and my manager were invited to explain the Wellness Recovery Action Plan (WRAP). We pointed out that many peers with mental health issues had WRAP manuals that the police officers could use to help with the crisis. Using a power point presentation, we familiarized the police with the WRAP. And, we passed around a couple of completed WRAP manuals for them to look through.

Also, during the week, the officers learn how to work with a person having a mental illness without escalating the crisis, as well as, ways of deescalating the crisis. Some peers shared their recovery story. It was an honor to participate in their training.

I do not know much to put in this text about the peers with whom I worked. I am not a psychiatrist. I tried not to judge them. I cared about them, even though I did not really know them. They were human beings that were hurting for a variety of reasons.

I got to know a little bit about those that were regular callers, though. Many talked about the lack of meaningful relationships in their lives. Some talked about crises in the relationships they had. Others talked about either the job they had, or the lack of a job. Some talked about their pet or their hobby. Some complained about the medications they had to take. Some talked about having nothing to give meaning to their lives. I had one that made a death threat against one of our peer support specialists. That one got into a lot of trouble. Some talked about health problems. There were those that felt hopeless and threatened self-harm or suicide. They all were people wanting to be heard. So, I actively listened with empathy, compassion and a sincere interest in their wellbeing.

As much as I cared about what I was doing, I had to leave Safe Harbor after about two years. The calls were becoming overwhelming, and I was beginning to experience burn out. The negative content of the calls, the length, those that called several times a shift, the urgency of some calls, all contributed to the stress. Most of the calls were from nice people. Some were vulgar, but that was extremely rare. I just could not keep up any longer. So, I left.

God is gracious.

# I WAS A PEER SUPPORT SPECIALIST

* * *

# 4 FRIENDSHIP PROGRAM

*God is gracious.*

After leaving Safe Harbor in August of 2014, I got a position as a peer support specialist with the Friendship Program, Inc... It had two sections, an adult day program, and a rehabilitation center for those with mental health issues. I was assigned to the rehabilitation center.

There were about ninety participants, and I was the only peer support specialist. I decided that I would go through the center and introduce myself to each of the participants, and, in the process, learn their names. I was not good at learning names, so I repeated their names as often as I could. It became a routine for me to greet each participant by their first name, as they arrived in the center. It was a routine that I maintained for as long as I was at the Friendship Program. I never regretted it.

The participants were very patient with me in my efforts to learn their names. It took me about six months to learn all of them. Then, as new people joined the program, I welcomed them to the program, and tried to learn their names as soon as possible.

Everyone was very kind to me. But, some were a bit leery of getting to know me. The program had two previous peer support specialists. One left after a few months. Another left after about a year. Some peers had allowed themselves to get close to them, and it hurt when the peer support specialists left. One participant I reached out to told me that they did not want peer support services for that very reason. I did not try to persuade them otherwise. As I have said, peer support services are voluntary. No one can be forced to accept peer support services. I respected their wishes and accepted them as they were. I was friendly with them, and, over time earned their respect. As time went by, some even eventually took advantage of peer support services.

Each day, I would make my rounds through the center, and engage in conversations with the participants. Slowly, I got to know them, and they got to know me. After a while, some would invite me to play card games with them. I did not know how to play cards, but that did not stop me. They were happy to teach me the card games they were playing. It paid off in the long run. We began to develop peer-to-peer relationships.

In addition to the connections that I was building, I worked with a program specialist staff member co-facilitating a Wellness Recovery Action Plan (WRAP) group. My co-facilitator took the lead, as I came up to speed with the group dynamics. It was not long before I was jumping in with both feet. The participants in the group were enthusiastic about the class.

Unfortunately for me and the participants, my co-facilitator took a position with another company several months later. That left me to facilitate the WRAP course by myself. Even so, I had a master's degree in education, and eight years teaching experience, so I was not totally unprepared for this situation. Dr. Copeland prefers that the WRAP course be facilitated by two trained facilitators, but one does what one can.

So, using Dr. Copeland's curriculum, I adjusted how I facilitated the course, since there would be only one facilitator. I introduced the course using Dr. Copeland's DVD that came with the curriculum guide. This gave the peers the opportunity to hear the story behind WRAP's beginnings, as well as an introduction to the WRAP itself, from the horse's mouth, as it were. I went to one of Dr. Copeland's websites, and printed copies of her articles that discussed each of the key concepts that were the foundation of the WRAP. We took turns reading the articles aloud and discussed them as a group. I then used her slide presentation to discuss the different parts of the WRAP. We shared our experiences of such things as triggers, early warning signs, and when things got worse. Then, in preparation for developing their workbook, we had discussions of activities and coping strategies that could be used as the wellness tools for their action plans, as Dr. Copeland noted in her texts. Then we would develop a personal WRAP for each peer in Dr. Copeland's WRAP workbook, using her red WRAP manual as a guide. We completed the Crisis Plan and reviewed the Post Crisis Plan. Finally, we would discuss slides that covered the various recovery topics.

Because we were only able to meet for two 45-minute periods one day a week, the course lasted about 12 weeks. That may seem like a long time, but the peers were determined to learn the material, develop their own WRAP, and put it into practice. After completing the course, I awarded them an achievement award printed on parchment paper. We made the presentation of the awards in front of the entire program body of peers. That way they received the recognition of their hard work that they had earned. I was very proud of them. Some who graduated the course swore by the WRAP. I think the good word of mouth press was why I tended to have a group waiting to take the course, as I was finishing up with the group before them.

I also assisted interested peers with the Region 6 Behavioral Healthcare scholarship application process to obtain scholarships that covered the costs of attending the annual three-day behavioral healthcare conference in Lincoln, Nebraska, including transportation there and back to Omaha. For many, this was their first time at the conference. I co-ordinated the logistics of getting the selected peers to Friendship with their luggage. The chartered bus was going to pick up the peers at Friendship around eleven o'clock the morning of the conference. Those who attended reported that they had such a good time that they were hoping to attend again the following year. After their return to Friendship, we sat down and wrote Thank You letters to the co-ordinator of the conference.

I, also, attended the conference. Friendship Program paid me to attend. Not to watch over the participants, but to attend the workshops on peer support topics for my professional development and required continuing education credits. The talks given by the keynote speakers were very interesting and enlightening. I was able to collect some valuable literature from the vendors that were there. There was a comfort room that gave fifteen-minute massages. I took advantage of that resource. Over all, the conference was a great success.

These were my activities for most of the first year at the Friendship Program. Slowly but surely the participants and I began to develop connections. I cared about each of the peers. I brought that and compassion to these relationships. I actively listened. And, I shared myself. I accepted them as they were and did not try to impose my ideas of what their recovery journey experience should be. I respected their worldview. And, at times, I shared some of my worldview to let them know that they were not alone in their struggles. I encouraged and affirmed them. I validated their experiences, as they shared some of their story.

I accepted their reality. I accepted that they might see and/or hear what I could not see or hear. And, I let them know that. But, I added that I had intrusive thoughts that at times were very scary. I shared that I struggled with the thoughts. We could connect on the fact that we each had our own mental health struggles. They seemed to appreciate that.

When major holiday seasons rolled around, I participated in the festivities. At Christmas and Thanksgiving, Friendship Program had special holiday meals for the participants. I would eat and socialize with the peers at those meals. They also had parties for the holidays. When I passed through any area where music was playing, I would pretend to be dancing. I did not really know how to dance, but it lightened things up, and the peers got a kick out of it. It helped to strengthen my relationships with the participants.

Staff also had potluck luncheons from time to time, such as when someone retired or were moving on to another career opportunity. With my wife's encouragement and help in coming up with a dish, I participated in the celebrations.

Once a year the Friendship Program would have an open house for the rehabilitation center, inviting guests of the participants, such as their family members and mental health providers. For privacy reasons, staff were not allowed to invite outside guests, such as one's spouse. Each of the staff members were assigned a different fundraising area, such as the raffle table, crafts table, pastries table, etc.

I was assigned the literature table. The materials were free to the attendees. I had several months advanced notice. So, I contacted the same online resources that I used to stock Safe Harbor's library. The table was covered with brochures about various mental illnesses, substance abuse, and trauma topics. I had some takers. In subsequent years, I researched a variety of topics online and printed the articles for the literature table, instead of the dated brochures.

But that was not all I did. I contributed one of my watercolor paintings to the raffle table. It was of a sunrise over the Sea of Galilee in Israel. It was very popular. An administrator stuffed the bag of raffle tickets and won the painting. She hung it in the hall until she retired and departed the Friendship Program, taking it with her. Each year that followed, I donated another watercolor painting for the raffle table.

During that first year I had some peers say that they felt that they were hearing the same thing in their groups that they had heard time and time again. They wished for more current data on the various mental illnesses. So, in response, I set up a reference table. I googled different mental health topics and printed out the articles I had researched. I made certain that I used reputable government sources, or agencies that were very well known for the quality of their work. I got ideas for research topics from the peers themselves, and from the topics of groups the program specialists were teaching. Sometimes staff would ask if they could have copies of the articles. I was happy to share.

The activities of Friendship were something new for me. But, I had made a commitment to myself that I was going to be more outgoing with these peers than I had been in the past. I was going to build a relationship with as many of the peers and staff as were open to it.

The first year I was at the Friendship Program that was pretty much all I did. The peers and I strengthened our peer-to-peer relationships, investing myself in them, and they are investing themselves in me. But, there was something missing in my heart, a fellow peer support specialist on the team.

Co-Supervision, later known as Co-Reflection, was a big part of my experience as a peer support specialist. When I first started peer support with The

# John Friday

Salvation Army I use to attend monthly Co-Supervision meetings conducted by the Region 6 Behavioral Healthcare manager of the Office of Consumer Affairs. We talked about a variety of things: somethings that were working for us, and somethings that were challenging for us. Then there was a topic for further discussion. I learned a lot, and I felt supported in my efforts to be the best peer support specialist I could be.

Later, at Safe Harbor, I had the privilege of meeting one-on-one with my manager, a pioneer of peer support in Nebraska, for Co-Supervision. As noted previously, we talked about what was going well with the four tasks of intentional peer support, and what were some of the challenges. I received feedback as to what he saw in my efforts at peer support. I not only felt validated, but I was enriched by his insights.

Then, at the Friendship Program, I felt isolated when it came to feedback about my peer support efforts from another peer support specialist's perspective. My supervisor tried to be supportive. She was happy with my activities as a peer support specialist. She thought that I did an outstanding job. I appreciated her support, but, it just was not the same. She was not a peer support specialist.

I sought out the perspective of the rehabilitation center's program manager. She, too, was appreciative of my work. We would discuss projects and groups that I wanted to implement. And, she would give me ideas of the activities she would like to see peer support implement. It was a good partnership. She was very much in favour of what a peer support specialist could bring to the table for the participants of her program.

I felt supported, but it still was not the same. They were not peer support specialists. I could not vent my frustrations or brainstorm aspects of my peer support activities, especially regarding the four tasks of intentional peer support. I could not call upon what they were observing first-hand about my experience of peer support. I could not question them about my evolving understanding of peer-to-peer relationships and the concept of "working toward". There was a void in my heart, but I carried on with what I was doing. The peers seemed to appreciate it, too.

There was more to peer support than conducting one-on-one peer support and facilitating groups. Region 6 implemented new data collection requirements for peer support. I began to document admissions to peer support services, as well as discharges from those services. Per their direction, I began to survey those discharged from peer services, answering questions about their satisfaction with the peer support they received. This data was then used to complete a performance indicator report for Region 6, which they used to track peer satisfaction with peer support services.

Soon after, the state of Nebraska implemented the Central Data System (CDS) to track behavioral healthcare services being used by individuals for which the state was being billed. I kept track of the peers I served in a Peer Support Log. At the end of each month, I identified those peers for whom the state was being billed. Then I completed the online CDS records for those individuals. I also documented those who had been receiving peer services but who declined peer support services for the given month.

There was also documentation of peer support services required by the Friendship Program's administration. I had to complete an activity sheet for each group that I facilitated, noting who attended. I would turn it in to the appropriate program specialist at the end of the day. In addition, I had to make an entry in each peer's chart that I met with one-on-one. Like with Safe Harbor, I noted why the peer met with me. For example, "The peer was having relationship issues." I documented what I did in response. For example, "This peer staff actively listened to, and empathize with the participant, as they shared some of their story. This peer staff shared some of his story, as it related to what the peer shared." Finally, I noted what the outcome was. For example, "The peer said that they felt better. This peer staff will touch base with the peer later." Then I recorded each name from both the groups and the individual one-on-one sessions in my monthly Peer Support Log. I also kept track in the log each day of the month on which we met. At the end of the month, I turned a copy in to my supervisor.

Besides my position with the Friendship Program, I was a peer support and wellness specialist trainer for the state. My supervisor at the Friendship Program let me take time off once a year to co-facilitate a forty-hour peer support and wellness specialist course offered by the state that led to certification of peer support and wellness specialists. Sometimes the course took place as a straight five-day week-long training period. Sometimes we met once a week for five weeks. The course was conducted by three trainers.

I got a lot out of teaching the course, both from listening to the other trainers' share, as well as listening to the perspectives and questions raised by the students. One learns a lot from teaching the subject matter. In preparing for the lessons, I had to have a clear understanding of what the curriculum wanted the students to take away from the lesson, as well as what I had learned about the material from personal experience in the field. I shared my lived experience of the topics in the discussions we had. I solicited the students' perspectives and questions on the topics. We had role play activities a lot, giving the students the opportunity to practice the skills being taught.

They were assigned to a group to work on a project to be presented on the last day of the course. The assignment was to demonstrate, in whatever way they chose, their understanding of the four tasks of intentional peer support. They could also include any other topics that were covered in the course. Some groups chose to do skits, or games, etc. After their presentations to the class, the rest of the students

John Friday

were given the opportunity to give positive feedback about what they liked about each of the participant's contribution to the project. Then the trainers did the same. Finally, each of the students was presented with a certificate of completion that qualified them to take the state exam for certification as a peer support and wellness specialist. I found it to be an exhausting, but very rewarding experience.

God is gracious.

\* \* \*

# 5 BANNER YEARS

*God is gracious.*

In the two and a half years that followed at Friendship, I added several new groups while continuing the groups and projects I started that first year: Region 6 Consumer Advisory Team, art journaling, art studio, and Pathways to Recovery.

I used to work with the Region 6 Behavioral Healthcare Consumer Affairs manager when we were both peer support specialists at The Salvation Army. He contacted me and invited me to join his Consumer Advisory Team (CAT). During my first meeting on the team, he noted that any peers I could bring to the meetings would be a welcome addition. So, I discussed the idea with my supervisor at the Friendship Program. She agreed to let me transport three of our participants to the meetings, if I had adequate automobile insurance on file and took the company's driver training. I complied with her terms.

I considered some peers at the center who were active in groups. I thought that they might bring that level of involvement to the CAT meetings. I approached three of the candidates and explained the situation. They were excited about the opportunity and accepted the manager's invitation.

The CAT meetings were held once a month on Monday afternoons. So, I transported the peers to the meeting and introduced them to the manager. He was delighted and so were they. All three new members of the team lived up to my expectations. They were very involved, and not shy about sharing their perspective. I was proud of them.

After the meetings I drove each of them home. They enjoyed their involvement on the team and became regular attendees. And, the manager was appreciative of their input on the team.

One of the projects that they discussed was a plan to nurture a sense of community for those with mental health issues called the Community Development Project. The idea was to form a committee of peers that would eventually take over operations, relieving Region 6 of any involvement.

## John Friday

The Community Development Project arranged such activities as Open Mic Night, where those with mental health issues gathered for a night of fun and socialization. This would help peers make new friends and show off their talents. Along with the entertainment was a display of artwork by artists who were also peers. I took advantage of the opportunity to loan a couple of my watercolor paintings for display. My wife and I also sat in the audience cheering on the peers that were brave enough to get up on stage and entertain us. It was a lot of fun.

The Community Development Project members also sponsored a picnic in one of the public parks in Omaha. We had a good turnout. Hotdogs, chili and hamburgers, along with an assortment of side dishes were provided. My wife and I brought three boxes of cream puff pastries. They were a hit. Peers socialized and played games. Pictures were taken. We all had a great time.

The members of the Community Development Project planned and put on the local first annual Sprout Conference. It was a behavioral healthcare conference like the one held in Lincoln, Nebraska, except that this one was held in Omaha. Also, the Sprout Conference was held for one day, instead of three. Like other conferences, there was a keynote speaker, and a variety of workshops. It was very good for its first year. I look forward to attending the next Sprout Conference.

After my first year at the Friendship Program, on the week prior to Veteran's Day, I found my thoughts turning to a young man I knew in the Philippines. He had been transferred to South Vietnam when the 1972 Easter Offensive broke out. While serving on a rescue mission, he was killed. I learned about it some years later when I ran into a friend of his. Now, my thoughts turn to him when I think of my time in the military, especially around Veteran's Day and Memorial Day. I become moody, quiet...reflective.

This time I decided to give art journaling a try in expressing what I was thinking and feeling. I contacted my old co-worker at Safe Harbor and asked if she would teach me the technical aspects of art journaling. She agreed. So, I met her at the Safe Harbor center. She noted that there were no rules. I used various art materials and old books to illustrate what was on my mind. I spent two hours letting my soul pour out onto the journal's pages. It was fitting that he be my first art journal entry. Since then I have used my art journal as a WRAP wellness tool. I have even taken extra steps in basing some of my watercolor paintings' compositions on some of my art journal's entries.

I decided that I would introduce art journaling as a group activity at the Friendship Program. After getting approval from my supervisor, I arranged to have it put on the monthly calendar of peer activities. I researched a little more about it online. I also bought a few books on the subject and put together a series of twelve lesson plans. I collected journaling prompts, old books, magazines and a variety of other art materials.

# I WAS A PEER SUPPORT SPECIALIST

I had a sign-up sheet for the first group, to get a committed group of truly interested parties. I did not want people dropping out of the group after brief entries in the art journals. We went through the lessons, giving the peers a solid guided experience of art journaling. I played soft meditative music in the background to set the mood. Several peers liked the experience, finding it helpful enough to continue using it months after completing the ten-week course.

About a year later, I had the opportunity to facilitate an art journal workshop at an annual behavioral healthcare conference in Lincoln, Nebraska. The title of the workshop was "Art Journaling: A Beginner's Consideration to Use as A Wellness Skill." I put together fifty tote bags of introductory materials. Well over sixty peers showed up. I had to turn people away. I used a power point presentation that I had put together for this workshop. I covered a brief history of art journaling, and, using slides of my own art journal's entries, took the participants through a hands-on activity of making entries into art journals of their own. We made two entries. Each had a selection of three prompts from which to choose. We spent 30 minutes each time journaling on their selected prompts. Afterwards, I got a lot of positive feedback. One peer support specialist told me that he was going to introduce art journaling to the peers that he serves.

About that same time, my supervisor at the Friendship Program and I discussed the idea of setting aside a scheduled time for anyone who wanted to participate in an art studio group. They would just spend some time expressing themselves creatively with art materials. It would not be a time for art lessons. Rather, it was just an opportunity for self-expression. One did not have to be an artist to participate.

I once again collected some quality art materials to make available to the peers. One could make a collage, various types of drawings (gel pen, or pencil), watercolor paintings (watercolor pencils, or watercolor paint kit), etc. One could also explore color, using adult design coloring books. Once again, I played a spectrum of soft meditative music in the background: Native American flute with sounds of nature; Asian strings and sounds of nature; Western European American piano, etc. Sometimes the room was packed, other times only a couple of peers would attend. That was okay. I still considered it a successful group.

Each year for about two years I was invited to exhibit my artwork as the "Artist of the Arboretum" in the Lincoln Regional Center administration building in Lincoln, Nebraska. Each time my supervisors gave me the day off to attend the opening. My work went on display for a month each time. In addition, since the peers could not leave their residence, I gave a power point presentation of my artwork to the peers in the women's facility, and then to the peers in the men's facility. The compositions of my paintings related to my lived experience of trauma and mental illness. I enjoyed sharing the story behind each piece of artwork. Each group thanked me for sharing my artwork with them. Then, at the 2015 Success, Hopes, and Dreams behavioral healthcare conference in Lincoln, I was presented with the 2015 Recovery Muse Award for my artwork. I was honored to receive it.

At the end of my first year at the Friendship Program, my supervisor talked with me about a group that she was interested in my facilitating. It was titled "Pathways to Recovery". It was a strengths recovery self-help curriculum developed by the University of Kansas School of Social Welfare, Office of Mental Health Research and Training. There was a workbook and accompanying group facilitator's guide.

I developed a thirty-six-page outline of the curriculum and shared it with my supervisor. She gave me the go ahead to implement the course. It was made up of four eleven-week modules. Module One covered the strengths recovery approach of the course, and the concept of recovery. Module Two developed the concept of the recovery journey and some of the challenges one could encounter. Module Three introduced life domains and guided the peers through setting goals for those domains. Then those goals were used as the basis for writing a personal recovery plan. Module Four discussed having a support system and guided the peer through the process of writing their personal recovery story.

The first group met on Tuesdays for one forty-five-minute session. The members of the group began to complain that it seemed that the discussion barely got going when the time was up. They wanted to meet for two sessions one day a week, for a total of ninety minutes. That way they could pick up where they left off from the morning session and continue the discussion in the afternoon. I encouraged them to each write down their request and place it in the suggestion box. I noted that the contents of the suggestion box were collected and read during the Tuesday team meeting. Once the issue came to the manager's attention, their request was granted.

Despite the course's length, the group became very popular. To meet the demand of individuals wanting to take the course, we opened additional groups on Thursdays and Fridays. Each group met once a week for ninety minutes. We would read aloud the readings for the day, and then discuss questions found in the workbook and facilitator's guide.

After gaining permission from the University of Kansas Office of Mental Health Research and Training, I developed a power point presentation for each of the modules to enhance the focus of the groups' discussions. The slides were a valuable aid to the discussion.

Peers noted that their attraction to the course was the quality of the discussions. Even though the groups tended to start with ten or twelve peers, a small percentage of them would drop out after the first module. For that reason, my supervisor did not want the peers writing in the workbooks until they reached module three. There were a lot of handouts for the first two modules, but modules three and four had very few handouts. The activities for the last two modules were found primarily in the workbook. After exploring and composing their own recovery story in module four, they were afforded the opportunity to share their story with others.

At the end of each of the four modules, the participants were presented a certificate of achievement for their hard work. The Pathways to Recovery certificates were awarded during a large group meeting of the entire peer community. Once a group completed the entire course, we celebrated with a DVD movie of their choice, as well as a large bag of gourmet popcorn and a cold drink for each peer.

The manager of Consumer Affairs at Region 6 Behavioral Healthcare approached me about contracting as a consultant to facilitate a Pathways to Recovery course for them. He had a group of hand-picked peers that he wanted to take the course. They were part of a group of leaders that were involved in helping to plan activities that would draw together a community of people with mental health and/or substance abuse issues. His desired outcome for this group of leaders was that, in participating in the discussions, they would get to know one another and bond together as a cohesive group. They had some truly great discussions, answering the questions on the power point slides, as well as from the workbook. Unlike the courses at the Friendship Program, Inc., the course at Region 6 met one evening a week for two hours.

At the completion of the course, they regularly met as Pathways to Recovery alumni. I was recently invited to a potluck dinner that they were having. It was nice to see old faces and catch up on their activities. I would say that the manager's intention was actualized.

My supervisor at the Friendship Program and I discussed possible groups that I might facilitate as a break from the WRAP group for a few weeks. We settled on a group titled "Exploring Wellness Skills: Looking for Additional Ways to Care for My Wellness". In this group, peers came together to share some of the strategies or skills that had been most effective in managing their wellness. The intent was to help each of us expand the options we have for managing our wellness by drawing upon the collective wisdom of our fellow peers.

We looked at the situations in which we used them. We examined the benefits that we experienced from using that skill. Finally, we shared our unique way of implementing that skill. We took notes on what we learned. It was a productive group.

Even I contributed to the discussions. I noted that, when I was triggered and got angry, I would inhale, as I clinched my fists at my side, then, as I slowly exhaled, I would relax my fists. I would do this until I calmed down. It was very effective. I was able to avoid a potentially bad situation becoming worse.

John Friday

    I enjoyed working with each of the groups. I learned a lot about myself, about relationships and the peers I served. The contributions of the participants in each of the groups were profound, reflecting the aims of the group.

    In the WRAP group, I watched the peers drink in Dr. Copeland's teachings about WRAP. Our shared hopes were that we would be better able to manage our symptoms to weather the storms of mental illness and live a better quality of life. In the art journaling class, I saw peers hopeful that journaling could become a wellness tool to express the pain they feel, getting relief to continue their journey. I watched the peers, using the art studio, delight in their own artistic creativity, expressing their thoughts and feelings on topics that moved their souls. In Pathways to Recovery, I listened to the profound insights each peer shared in their responses to the questions raised about the recovery journey and the challenges encountered along that winding road. In the group that explored the wellness skills used by other peers, I witnessed a willingness to risk being vulnerable so that someone else could benefit from their experience.

    I learned a lot about recovery. That it is a journey, rather than a destination. I have learned that I have been on this journey for quite some time. I began to see the journey as a key element of the "working toward" of peer support. We each have different goals in our recovery journey, unique to who we are. We grow as we progress along the recovery path, getting closer to our goals. Each time we actualize a goal a new goal calls to us, goals that the recovery journey moves us toward. It is not always an easy path to travel. Relapse is not the end, but an expected part of the journey. The rewards make it a worthwhile trek.

    God is gracious.

* * *

# 6 SEASONED VOCATION

*God is gracious.*

I was not a therapist. I was not a counselor. I was not a social worker. I was not a psychiatrist. I was a peer support and wellness specialist and there was a big difference.

I became a peer support specialist in September of 2010. As I said before, I started out without any specialized training. I did not even know what peer support was. It is a situation that many newly starting out peer support specialists find themselves. It was a job. Although it was a job like none I had ever had before. Instead of hiding the fact that I had mental illnesses, they not only wanted me to be open about my illnesses, they required it.

So, when I started I made a commitment to myself and the peers I was serving that I would find a way to provide them with the best peer support service that I could muster. In addition, each morning, on the way to work, I would pray to be the peer support specialist the peers needed me to be. Over time, peer support became more than a career. It became a vocation.

I was excited when the opportunity arose to take Nebraska's peer support and wellness specialist training designed by Shery Mead. It was a major influence on the kind of peer support services I provided. Over the years the lived experience of implementing Shery Mead's peer support model has had a profound impact on me and my journey as a peer support specialist.

I invested myself in planning the group activities and collected quality materials that I frequently paid for out of my own pocket. I wanted the peers to have a positive and rewarding experience of the activity. On occasion I developed power point presentations to enhance the experience of the group discussions. The peers appreciated my efforts; I received a lot of affirmations.

The peers were often hurting and depended upon the listening ear of the peer support and wellness specialist to empathize with them and validate their experiences. For many we were the first person who they felt truly understood what they were going through. Not because we have a specialized education, but because we have lived experience. As I shared earlier, I have had peers say that they shared with some peer support specialists things that they would not share even with their family or mental health provider. They feared that these individuals just would not have understood.

For some, they had the unfortunate experience of trying to share themselves with those they cared most about, only to have that person or persons rebuke them, telling the peer to "just get over it." Or, they would say things, like "All you need to do is get a job! You will do better then." "Don't be such a wimp! Everybody has problems." "Pull yourself up by your bootstraps!" "You are just lazy!" "Nothing is wrong with you that a good day's work won't fix!" "There is no such thing as mental illness! It's just your imagination." "All of that medication you take is your real problem!" Some people's ignorance and bias are earthshaking. The stories the peers tell of their experiences with opening to people who do not have mental illnesses is, at times, more cruel than having a mental illness.

Again, knowing that had encouraged me to push myself to be the best peer support and wellness specialist I could be. And, that meant taking responsibility for my growth as a peer support specialist. It was an issue so important to peer support that Nebraska included it as part of their Peer Support Specialist Code of Ethics.

I attended conferences where I took advantage of the workshops presented for state required professional development. For my own edification, I researched and studied online articles on various mental health topics, like intentional peer support, WRAP key concepts, mental illnesses, etc… I read books on ways WRAP and peer support could work together for the benefit of the peers I served.

I learned to actively listen. When I say "actively" I mean that I did not spend time while they were sharing to think of what I was going to say in response. I sat with silence, no matter how uncomfortable it felt, with the understanding that it gave the peer an opportunity to reflect on their feelings, formulate their thoughts, and ponder for themselves about what they were sharing, and about the peer support experience.

I did not make assumptions. I never knew whether, or not the peer sitting before me had experienced some trauma or not. There were no outward signs saying, "This peer was raped." Or, that peer was molested as a child. Nor, that this other peer was humiliated by being handcuffed by police in front of their family or neighbors. So, I treated each peer as though there was a good possibility that they had a traumatic background. If they opened and shared some traumatic experience, I listened respectfully and let them lead the conversation. I did not pry but accepted what they were willing to share as a sacred trust. Confidentiality was a must and an ethical requirement of the position.

# I WAS A PEER SUPPORT SPECIALIST

Actively listening meant making certain that I really understood what they were communicating. I parroted back what I heard, so that they knew that I was there with them. I asked clarifying questions to give them the chance to correct my understanding. And, I used my body language to communicate my interest and attentiveness to what they were sharing. I let them know that I was there with them; that I was there for them. I cared. And, because I sincerely cared, I pushed myself.

I had a compulsion to make it to work, even when I might not have been having so great a day myself. I might even have shared that with a peer, so that they could experience the giving side of the relationship in empathizing with me. But, I never went into the gory details. It was not my aim to trigger them, or dump on them.

Peer support is a partnership. Together we nurture our relationship, for the sake of the relationship. Because, as we strengthen that relationship, we become invested in it. That is the point. In that relationship we learn of other ways of seeing the world that also sheds light on how we view the world. We learn that our vision is not the only vision of how the world operates. Together we challenge ourselves to re-examine why we believe the way we believe. We grow in our respect for the other person's worldview, while respecting our own view. Together, we are on a journey of not only self-discovery, but of learning about each other.

As a peer support specialist, it was incumbent upon me to maintain ethical behavior. There have been times when peers, meaning well, and in appreciation for the services they received, tried to give me gifts. I politely thanked them for the gift but explained that I could not accept it. I noted that a card would be a nice memento. Often the peer was happy to oblige.

In addition, protecting the peer's privacy was also an ethical consideration. Part of that was not talking about them, especially outside the workplace and not even to my spouse. But, it also meant sharing professionally on a need to know basis. Not gossiping. What was said between us was confidential.

Also, to protect their privacy, if I encountered a peer outside of the program, I did not acknowledge them. That is, unless they first acknowledged me. For some peers it was not public knowledge that they were receiving mental health services. And, they wanted it to stay that way. I experienced both situations.

Like some people, I might not have felt all that great on a given day. I took care of myself, too. Taking care of myself was taking care of the relationship. Sometimes I was the one having a mental health issue. Just because I was a peer support specialist, did not mean that I was invulnerable to the storms of mental illness.

Like I said, what qualified me to be a peer support specialist was the fact that I had a lived experience of mental illness. However, it was an ongoing lived experience. Sometimes I shared some of that story, as it related to what the peer was sharing. It created and strengthened a connection and sent the message that they were not alone in their experience.

I worked my WRAP. Just like I encouraged others to work their WRAP. Sometimes it was me who needed to take a 45-minute break at work to call a warm line, like Safe Harbor. Or, if not them, then perhaps calling a peer support specialist friend, or mentor. If needed, letting my supervisor know how I was doing and taking off the rest of the day. If I do not take care of myself, what kind of role model of the recovery journey am I? I do not take my responsibilities lightly. And, I made certain that, if I needed a break, I in fact needed a break.

On some occasions in the morning, I would rather roll over in bed and go back to sleep. Not because I was tired but because I felt down and had a lack of energy. Then I pushed myself to go into work, because I knew that if I stayed at home I would isolate. And, that could deepen my bout of depression. Going to work to be among my peers was just the medicine that I needed. Peers were very supportive of my wellbeing, too.

There have been peers who have expressed the same attitude and push needed to come in to program. Some peers told me that sometimes the only thing that got them out of the house and into program was a group in which they were invested. On some occasions the experience of a group would draw into program even an individual who had agoraphobic issues.

I watched peers new to the program sit in the day room off by themselves, not responding to any passer-by that might greet them, including myself. Months passed before one might catch them smile or grunt in response to a similar greeting. It might be almost a year before one saw them stake out a cubby hole in the community room during a large group gathering, as they watched the proceedings unfold, still not talking. They may never attend small group gatherings. Then again it may just take time, and some soul not giving up on greeting them by name with a smile. One just does not know the power of a smile, or the impact one may have on another soul.

Not every aspect of a peer support specialist's day was exciting. There were mundane tasks that needed to be done, like paperwork and updating the records of the peers you served. Peer support was not generally free to anyone but the peer themselves. There were a variety of funding resources and each had various documentation requirements. They wanted to know that they were getting the services for which they paid. It could be Medicaid, federal resources, other state resources, grants, foundations, donations from the community or some benevolent philanthropic soul.

Generally-speaking, peer support specialists do not make a lot of money. I know that when I was first hired my hourly wage was only $10.00 dollars an hour.

On top of that my job was only part-time. Lucky for me, I got to work twenty hours per week. I was also fortunate that I had compensation coming in on a monthly-basis from the Veteran's Administration for a service connected disability. My mental healthcare was also supplied by the Veteran's Administration.

Some peer support specialists were able to make ends meet because they had a Social Security Disability income. For most of them it was the only way that they could afford to pay for their psychiatric medications, and doctor's bills. Those with severe mental health issues often had as many or more than a dozen different medications prescribed for them. The cost of just one medication could sometimes be several hundred dollars just for a 30-day supply. When I was first prescribed the anti-depressant Luvox, I was told that a one-month supply cost over $400.00 dollars.

I knew one peer support specialist co-worker who the Social Security Administration would only allow to work about sixteen hours a week, or she would lose her disability benefits. One might think that if one got a full-time peer support specialist position they would get medical benefits. But those days had changed. One company for whom I worked did away with all medical benefits. As a result, several employees went to work for other companies where benefits were much reduced, but they at least had some medical benefits, if only for themselves and not their spouse.

The program specialists that took their place had less experience but were receptive to not having medical benefits. Although, it must be said that the new staff members did bring in new perspectives, and new ways of doing things. As for peer support specialists, they sometimes must be very creative with their budget to make ends meet.

As a peer support specialist, I served individuals who, like myself, had been diagnosed with a variety of psychiatric labels: bipolar I/II disorder, obsessive-compulsive disorder, schizophrenia, schizoaffective disorder, borderline personality disorder, or others. Many had more than one or two labels.

But peer support was not about diagnosis and labels. Rather, it was about lived experiences and the feelings and thoughts generated around those experiences. It was about relationships that were sometimes tainted by stigma. Or, as we learned in Pathways to Recovery, it was even about self-stigma. It was about trauma and loss. It was about regaining hope and moving toward a higher quality of life. It was, as Dr. Copeland taught, learning that they were the experts on themselves.

Recovery was holistic. While we studied the course Pathways to Recovery, each peer explored their life domains, setting goals that they wanted to work toward in their recovery journey. That was true for me, too. There was more to my life than peer support. And, those other areas impacted my recovery journey.

John Friday

The Pathways to Recovery course was itself a journey of self-discovery. The discussions and insights shared by the peer participants helped me better understand the "moving toward" task of Shery Mead's intentional peer support model. I went from seeing peers as broken souls to being fellow travellers at different points along the unique road of their recovery journey.

I found that a good many peers would like to join the workforce. Some expressed a desire to become a peer support specialist. And some would make great peer support specialists.

However, one does not have to become a peer support specialist just because one has mental health issues, and/or substance abuse challenges. There are other jobs that one could do well. I know a peer who completed peer support training and then realized that it was not something that they wanted to do after all. So, instead of defaulting to peer support, find that thing for which one has a passion and do that. I know of peers who have careers in fields other than peer support and do very well.

That said, for me peer support is a rewarding vocation. I get to meet brave souls that push themselves to weather the storms of mental illness and strive toward a life that is personally fulfilling. They do not wallow in self-pity but muster up the courage to be a better person. They have their good days and their not so good days. But they know that, as bad as some days are, better days are coming. And, because of their struggles, they can be there for their friends. They are compassionate and supportive. What some see as an unfortunate burden, I see as the instrument of their self-growth. And, because I share in that struggle, there is hope for me, too. They are my role models, my heroes.

God is gracious.

* * *

# 7 MENTAL HEALTHCARE

*God is gracious.*

Part of my lived experience of mental illness includes the mental health system. I bring that experience to my peer support relationships with the peers I serve. My earliest experience of mental health providers goes back to when I was in junior high school.

My parents had a volatile relationship. When I was about nine years old my dad kicked us out of the house and married a young lady with five kids. As my mom later described it, she woke up one morning to a shotgun pointed to her head and my dad demanding that she leave, taking the two children. That would be me and my younger brother.

In any case, we first moved from the farm to government housing in a nearby town. Later, we moved to Houston, Texas where my mom got a better job. In fact, she got a couple of them to make ends meet.

It was while I attended school there that my junior high school art teacher took an interest in a pencil drawing that I had done. Its composition was a bit on the dark side. It was a portrait of a drifter standing in a back alley with skyscrapers forming the background. My teacher set up an easel and canvas. She supplied me with her oil paints and brushes. After I finished doing an oil painting from the drawing, she showed it to my mom.

In turn, my mom took me to see a psychiatrist at a children's hospital in Houston. He showed me ink blots, and a variety of photographs. He had me tell stories about what I saw in them. Then he set me on an amphitheatre stage in front of an audience of people in white coats. It was a sort of show and tell. I showed them my artwork and talked about my compositions. I answered their questions. Then it was over. My mom took me home and never talked about it. And, I was too young to question what it was all about. One simply did what adults told you to do.

A couple of years later she placed me in a home for boys. She said that she could no longer afford to feed me. I continued to draw. The other boys liked the drawings I did. I stayed pretty much to myself and tried to stay out of trouble by obeying the adults and keeping a low profile.

I started withdrawing and sleeping in school. I had just begun high school and I was so far behind that I could not keep up. I could not comprehend the material.

Evidently, the director of the home for boys told my mother. She showed up and took me to a local psychologist who worked out of his home. He gave me an I.Q. test. I did well on it, he said. He never asked me any questions during our sessions. Instead, I lay on his couch while he sat across from me in an arm chair. I slept through our entire time together. Then, on one occasion, mom asked me what we did. I told her. She hit the roof. That was the last time I saw that psychologist. Again, she did not share with me what he said, or why she even took me to see him. So, I just forgot about it and continued to sleep in my classes at school.

I flunked my way through high school, drawing and sleeping in class. I was pretty much passed along from grade level to grade level. I guess my teachers figured that I would graduate and become a full-time artist. Perhaps they thought that I would hang out with the hippies in California. I do not know what was on their minds.

After graduation, mom reminded me that the Vietnam Conflict/War was going full swing. To avoid being drafted and sent to die in some rice paddy, I enlisted in the Air Force. I developed a habit of volunteering for any assignment that came up. By doing so, I travelled a lot. I hardly did any drawings at all any more.

But, I had some interesting adventures, including having a bar girl in the Philippines put a contract on me to have me killed. She was upset that I had dropped her to go out with another bar girl. To protect me, the second bar girl took out a contract on her so that, if anything happened to me, she would be dead before nightfall. It worked. The first bar girl dropped the contract on me. Even so, I came out of the Philippines with the shakes. Violent crime was a way of life there.

I not only served in the Philippines, Thailand, and Florida, I travelled on missions to Guam, Kwajalein Island, Midway Island, Japan, and Okinawa. I worked as a crew chief on HC-130 rescue aircraft. I later became an aircrew member on AC-130 gunships.

The gunship I was on flew cover for the evacuation of the United States embassy in Phnom Penh, Cambodia in 1975. After the fall of the pro American government, it was like a wall of silence was erected. No one came out of Cambodia, and no word was heard about what was going on inside the country. At that time, we had no idea of what later was referred to as the "Killing Fields" of Cambodia.

I watched people, fleeing from South Vietnam as the war collapsed, virtually rain from the skies in Thailand in all sorts of aircraft. Once they landed they became refugees held in aircraft hangers. No one wanted to take them in, and Thailand did not want to keep them. They were still there when I shipped back home to the United States.

I did a lot. I saw a lot. When I got back to the U.S., I was stationed at Andrews Air Force Base in Maryland, just outside Washington, D.C... This time I worked support as a ground crew maintenance member. It gave me the opportunity to attend a local community college part-time.

Most of my youth I was a failure. Or, at least, that was what I was told. This time I wanted to find out for myself. I enrolled in psychology and English classes. I earned high marks, "A's" and "B's". I was bitten by the academic bug. I signed up for a full load...while I was still working a 40-hour week for the Air Force. It was not long before I had a mental breakdown and became suicidal.

As I entered the base, coming from class, I approached a fork in the road. The path to the left passed a large tree. The path to the right led to the base hospital. I knew that, if I took the road to the left, I would slam on the gas pedal and ram my car into the tree. I chose the road to the left and went to the hospital.

Going inside the hospital, I was met by a clerk. He said that sick-call for military troops was over. Now it was time for military dependents. I explained the situation and he put me in an examination room. Soon after, a psychiatrist showed up. I shared my story. He prescribed an antidepressant. I took it and was soon feeling no pain. He arranged to see me as an outpatient. I was given a few days off to let me rest and give the medication time to work its magic.

With the doctor's guidance, I dropped all but one of my courses. He wanted me to keep one class. I think so that I would not see myself as a failure. I did well in that class, and in other classes I later took. This time no more than two courses at a time. It made me want to get out of the Air Force and attend college full time. But, I still had time on my enlistment, so I was going to have to wait. In the meantime, as I noted, I took a lighter academic load.

I met with my psychiatrist once a week in his office at the hospital. Mostly, we talked about how I was doing on the medication, and how I was doing in school. He told me that I had major depression. I did not really understand what that meant, and he did not explain. He also had me going to group therapy once a week at the hospital. It was interesting. There were men and women in the group. I did not say anything for a while. I not only did not know what to say, but I was also a bit withdrawn. Weeks passed into months. The other members of the group were very supportive. I became more relaxed and started participating more in group.

Then the President of the United States decided that he was going to cut back on the number of troops that served in the military. The Vietnam Conflict/War had ended and the number of troops in the service were no longer needed. As troops were discharged, there would be a reshuffling of the remaining troops regarding the bases where they were stationed. Some bases would be closed over time.

## John Friday

I was chosen to be reassigned to a squadron in Virginia. The problem was that, according to military regulations, a troop had to have at least a year left on his enlistment to be transferred. I only had nine months left on my enlistment. So, the Air Force wanted me to reenlist, so that they could transfer me to this new duty station. I politely declined.

I saw this as my opportunity to get out of the service, and enroll full-time in a college in Houston, Texas. I wanted to study for the priesthood, but I did not know what degree I wanted to earn. I just wanted to go to college full-time.

When my psychiatrist learned of this, he became very sober. He kept emphasizing to me that I needed to make sure that I continued seeing a doctor after I was discharged from the Air Force. For some reason I just did not understand what the big deal was. I did not want to harm myself anymore. I had been seeing the doctor and going to group for the past six months. Wasn't it time to end this whole thing? Wasn't I cured? This was my train of thought, but I never said a word about it to the doctor. That pretty much was how things were when I was discharged and went back to Houston.

One of the last things I was told during my discharge process was to make certain that I went to the V.A. hospital when I got home and had a physical exam done. That way, if something was found, it could be identified as a service connected condition. One of the things I learned in the military was to follow orders. So, I went.

When I went to the V.A. hospital in Houston for my exam, I assumed that they were there to help me. No one prepares you for what you are going to experience when you get there. I was never asked about the mental health issues that I had at Andrews Air Force Base. They handed me some papers to complete, never explaining the forms and the kind of things I should be concerned about. The thing that was on my mind at the time was my jaw.

During one of my assignments overseas, I had a dentist pull one of my wisdom teeth that was hurting. As a result, I got dry socket from the extraction. On top of that, my jaw started popping whenever I ate. It turned out that I could now dislocate my jaw at will. It had never been like that before the tooth was pulled. I was not certain as to what could be done, but I included that in the paperwork the V.A. gave me.

A V.A. dentist took x-rays of my jaw. First, with my jaw dislocated. Then with it back in place. He told me that there was no way to prove that the condition of my jaw being able to dislocate at will did not exist prior to my enlistment. As a result, my claim was denied.

Instead, I was awarded ten percent disability for hemorrhoids. Something for which I did not even file a claim. So, they must have reviewed my medical records. The way I took it was that the V.A. was saying that I was not a perfect asshole. As for the diagnosis of major depression, no mention was made of it. And, I had forgotten all about it. As a result, I fended for myself.

I did not stay in the seminary very long. I attended the University of St. Thomas in Houston, and soon met a girl there. I began to court her, and it was not long before we were engaged.

However, there were some things about my behavior that concerned her. For example, on one occasion on campus I had an emotional outburst and slammed my fist into an iron girder that was holding up an elevated walkway. It rang loud enough that professors stepped out of their classrooms to see what was happening.

On another occasion, she was sitting behind me on the couch, as I sat on the floor working on a watercolor painting. She was feeling hot, so she turned the fan toward us to cool things off. But, I started having difficulty with manipulating the paint. Then I realized that the fan was blowing on it. I jumped up in a rage and raced to the fan, kicking it across the room. She was sitting dead still, afraid to move. I did not say anything to her.

She talked to me about my mental health. If we were to get married, she insisted that I first seek help from a mental health provider. I could not afford to see a psychiatrist, so I went to an agency called Interface. They had a sliding scale fee for people like me. I was assigned a social worker. We met once a week and talked. I do not even remember about what. I just wanted to fix things so that I could marry the young lady.

At one point the social worker recommended that I start taking psychiatric medication to help regulate my mental health symptoms. I could barely afford her fee, how was I supposed to afford psychiatric medications. She referred me to a research agency where I signed up for a clinical study. I received medication free of charge. However, I never knew if I was getting the medication being tested or the placebo.

This went on for about a year. Then I became impatient. I confronted my social worker, wanting to know when I was going to be cured. She seemed surprised by my question. She went on to explain that I was emotionally disturbed, and that I would never be "cured". Rather, I would be on an ever-expanding cycle outward. Every now and then I would encounter some event that would throw me into the middle of my emotional gunk, and I would explode. I was stunned. I told her that I would not wish that off on a dog. And, I left.

I drove to a Jesuit retreat house in Louisiana to confront God and get healed. That did not turn out as planned, either. After three days and a temper tantrum before God, I was resolved to my emotional fate. I drove back to Houston and shared with my fiancée that I could not change. As a result, we broke up.

I decided to give the seminary another try. But, after a few years of being in and out of the seminary, I went to work for an insurance company in Houston. They trained me to be a custom home appraiser. I would evaluate the home and determine a replacement value for it, in case some tragic event destroyed it. I was pretty good at it.

I met a young lady at work and, after dating for about six months, we got married. I used to tell her stories of my time teaching in a parochial school as a seminarian. She encouraged me to become a teacher. So, I earned a master's degree in education and got a teaching certificate. Soon after, I started teaching fifth grade in an elementary school.

At the same time, we were trying to get pregnant. After about three years we finally had a little boy. I was madly in love with him. However, after eight years of marriage, she and I broke up. She was originally from Nebraska and returned to her hometown to be with her family.

I was a teacher on contract with a school district in Houston, so I could not leave immediately. I started having emotional problems from being separated from my son. I arranged to visit my son in Nebraska. I knew no one there. My former sister-n-law said that I could stay in a room in her home during my visit. I made the 950-mile trip to see him.

Then something happened, and my ex-wife refused to let me see my son. I did not understand why. I soon learned that he had told her that he wanted to go live with me. She blew up, thinking that I put him up to it. I had not. I noted that he was barely five years old. He does not know what he wants. But, she still would not let me visit him.

I left in a rage. I drove nonstop back to Houston. During the 18 hour drive I obsessed about ways to take my vengeance out on my ex-wife. As I got closer to the city I began having thoughts of self-harm. I was driving in front of three 18-wheelers when I started having the compulsion to flip my steering wheel, causing the car to wreck with the trucks.

All I could do was yell "No! No! No!" I did not know what else to do than go to the V.A. hospital for help.

I entered the hospital and approached the registrar. I explained what I was feeling. He told me that he was not sure that he would be able to get me in to see a doctor. He directed me to have a seat, while he investigated it. I sat along the wall. I became anxious and confused as to what else I could do if they refused to help me.

Suddenly there was a rush of people around me. I was quickly ushered into the emergency room and seated in a chair in the middle of an examination room. It was not long before a psychiatrist arrived. He asked me if I was aware that I had started pounding the back of my head into the wall. I was not. He said that they would give me a supply of an antidepressant.

The doctor went on to say that I did not want to be admitted to the psychiatric ward. He said that it was not a nice place to be. He referred me to the Vet Center across town. I did not care, if I got some help.

The Vet Center was indeed nice. They assigned me a psychiatric social worker. He administered a psychiatric exam. We then developed a treatment plan.

The social worker advised me to stop taking the medication the psychiatrist gave me. It was known that the medication eventually caused ticks in the face that would not go away, even if one stopped taking it. I stopped taking the medication in question immediately.

One of the activities on my treatment plan was herbal tea therapy. It was the first time I had ever experienced an alternative therapy. The herbal tea was relaxing. I continued to visit the Vet Center for about a year. That is, until I moved to Nebraska to be near my son. I was not going to do to my son what my own father did to me.

My social worker advised me to contact the Vet Center in Nebraska and they might be able to help me. In the meantime, there was the alternative tea therapy that we had been using. I thanked my social worker for all the help he had given me, and I left for Nebraska.

God is gracious.

* * *

# 8 THE NEBRASKA FACTOR

*God is gracious.*

I arrived in Nebraska June 1st, 1994. Things not only did not go as planned, I was totally unprepared for what did happen.

At first, I sent out fifty resumes a week for several weeks for various teaching positions. I had a master's degree in education and eight years teaching experience in Texas. I had high hopes for getting a job. I did not get one interview. After six months I became very discouraged and could not understand why I was not getting called.

I was running low on funds, so I started taking low paying odd jobs. They barely paid the bills. Fortunately for me my son was only five. Taking him to public parks to play was fine with him. I also had a collection of VHS children's movies that he found entertaining. So, I was doing pretty good.

Still, jobwise I was becoming pretty stressed out and discouraged. But, I was committed to not leaving Nebraska. My son was here, and I was determined to stay to be with him.

Finally, in the autumn of 1995 I saw an ad for a parochial junior high school teacher. I interviewed for the position and was hired on condition that I completed the requirements for certification. It turned out that I needed to retake two teaching courses before Nebraska would issue a teaching certificate.

I enrolled in two master's courses at a local university to get my teaching credentials from Nebraska. I had taken the courses in Texas, but Nebraska did not accept them. I was required to retake the courses. I should have taken them at the undergraduate level. They would have served just as well. The courses were demanding and added to the stress I was experiencing.

I was responsible for seventh grade homeroom and math. I also taught sixth and eighth grades math. It turned out that the eighth-grade math class ran off the seventh-grade homeroom teacher. The seventh graders liked her a lot. They were not happy to see me. They were committed to forcing me out, too. They were a source of discipline problems that I did not have with the sixth and eighth graders.

After several months, I started feeling myself slipping into a cold dark place. I felt overwhelmed and low on energy. I went to see a psychiatrist. He prescribed a medication for me to take. It had no effect. It was like taking sugar pills.

Finally, one morning before class I had a run-in with the parents of one of the seventh-grade students. The father began yelling. The Principal became involved. Then the pastor got involved. I had enough. So, I resigned on the spot.

The mental anguish was unbearable. I did not have the strength to continue. I was in a deep dark cold hopeless abyss. It seemed to make sense to me to escape the pain through suicide. I was no longer thinking rationally.

In the past, two things had kept me from taking my life. First was the fear of being damned to Hell. The other was the concern for my son and the impact my suicide would have on him.

I reasoned that I was made for Hell. That removed that obstacle. I decided to tell my ex-wife that, if anything happened to me, she was to tell my son that I had been killed in a car wreck. That would remove the second obstacle.

I continued to tie up loose ends by purchasing a CD player that played five CDs. My intention was to overdose on sleeping pills. Playing five CDs would provide enough music to see me into oblivion. The music would be performed by new age artist Enya. I had become a fan when I listened to it playing in the psychiatrist's waiting room at the behavioral healthcare clinic.

Then I called my ex-wife and delivered the intended message. She did not agree but asked me to see my pastor. I agreed to do as she wished.

While I was driving over to the church office, my ex-wife called my pastor and expressed her concern. After I arrived in his office, we talked about my intentions for over an hour. Nothing changed on my part by the end of our conversation. I left for home, and he called the 911 operator. By the time I got home the police were waiting for me.

As soon as I saw the officer I knew why he was here. I told him that it was true. He asked what was true. I responded that I was going to kill myself. He said that he could not let me do that. I could not understand why. I began to reassure him that it was okay. The officer calmly explained what he was doing as he gently placed me in handcuffs. I did not mind. He noted that it was for my and his safety.

This experience of police officers responding to a suicide call became a significant part of my worldview. Years later, as a peer support specialist, this would be a part of my story that I shared with my peers, especially when I talked about the Crisis Intervention Team (CIT). It was a different perspective than those of some of my peers. Some shared how they felt humiliated by being handcuffed in front of their family and/or neighbors. For me, how the police officer handled my suicide call only made sense. I appreciated their compassion and professionalism. Even as my peers and I shared differing views, we respected and accepted that difference.

The police officer was unable to locate a hospital with psychiatric services in Omaha that had an available bed. The only one with an open bed was across the river in Council Bluffs, Iowa. For that reason, they called my pastor and requested that he drive me to the emergency room there. My pastor agreed to oblige.

I was in the hospital for ten days. Throughout that time, I had racing thoughts of ways to kill myself. They were nonstop. The medication I was given did not help. The doctor assigned to me told me that he did not think that I had obsessive-compulsive disorder (OCD). Finally, leaning across his desk, he shook his finger at me, saying, "Stop thinking like that!" Despite the continued thoughts of self-harm, I was discharged from the hospital.

After leaving the hospital, I took my son on an outing to the zoo in Omaha. He enjoyed it. As we were wandering around the exhibits, I saw a man that reminded me of the man who had yelled at me. I could not be sure. So, I followed him, trying to figure out if it was indeed him. My intention was to beat him to a pulp, putting him in the hospital. Consequences be damned. I just could not be sure, so I gave up. I took my son back to his mother, and then headed home myself.

As I approached my apartment building, a young man about in his twenties passed by me. I began stalking him. I followed him all the way to his apartment. I did not do anything. He went into his apartment, and I went to mine, which was on a different floor. I had become a danger to others.

The next day I had an appointment with my therapist. I decided that I would do a blood painting, using my blood. I placed a kitchen knife into my day timer, picked up my sketchpad, and heading out the door to my appointment.

I walked into my therapist's office. She saw the sketchpad and asked me what was going on. I told her of my intention and that the knife was in my day timer. She took my day timer. Removing the knife and putting it in her desk drawer, she sent me back to the hospital emergency room.

After I was admitted to the adult psychiatric ward of the hospital, I shared with the doctor the incidents at the zoo, and at the apartment building. I do not remember the doctor saying anything. I kept to myself.

I sat on a couch that was in an area connected to the hall. The nurse's station was at the intersection of the adult and adolescent wards. A man was yelling at the nurse in the nurse's station, evidently about the treatment his son was receiving. He reminded me of the father who yelled at me. I was immediately triggered and slammed my fist into the coffee table that was in front of me. Nurses came from everywhere. I was rushed into the quiet room and five-point restrained. Then one of the nurses injected me with a medication. I quickly passed out.

Much later, I received a bill from Douglas County Hospital in Omaha. My insurance had run out, so I was sent there for observation. I have no memory of my stay. The bill was the only evidence I had of being there.

I woke up from being drugged in the Veteran's Administration (V.A.) Medical Center in Omaha. I had been taken off all medication so that they could get a baseline of my condition. Again, my mind was flooded with thoughts of ways to kill myself. I asked a nurse for a tablet and a pencil. She gave them to me, and I began writing in detail what I was experiencing with my thoughts.

The main psychiatrist came in to the examination room with his entourage of resident doctors and talked to me about what was going on with me. I was very upset with my experience of doctors so far. In the heat of my emotions I began telling him about everything that had been going on in my head. I noted that, even in that moment, I was thinking of going into the hall, bending over, and running the length of the hall, ploughing my head into the wall at its end.

I told him that I did not care if he did electro-shock, or a lobotomy, or whatever. I just wanted him to make the thoughts stop. He assured me that he would be able to help. Then he and the other doctors went out into the hall.

One of the resident doctors stepped back into the room. He introduced himself and said that, if I was willing, he would be my doctor. He would be working with me as an outpatient. I agreed. He said that once I was released from the hospital we would meet on a weekly basis. He said that we would discuss it more later. Then he left.

After a few days I was moved from the psychiatric intensive care unit (PICU) to the main ward. I spent about ten days as an inpatient in the V.A. hospital, and then was discharged.

Within a week I was seeing the resident as both my doctor and my therapist. The medication they prescribed began to work. The thoughts of self-harm began to taper off. Eventually, I would just have occasional nuisance thoughts. I learned to dismiss them and refocus my mind on other things.

The doctor shared the diagnosis of what was happening with me. My primary diagnosis was major depression. There were two other diagnoses that complicated my condition: obsessive-compulsive disorder (OCD), and borderline personality disorder. I was given permission to visit the medical library, where I researched these diseases in the DSM-III to learn more about them and what they meant for me.

Not long after my discharge from the hospital, I received a letter from the V.A. directing me to travel to Lincoln, Nebraska to meet with a psychiatrist who was going to give me an evaluation. Once there I spent the morning with him. He gave me tests, and we talked.

John Friday

He told me that he had reviewed my military medical records and learned that I had been diagnosed in the Air Force with major depression. He asked me why the doctors in Houston did not grant me a service connected disability for this condition, especially since it was in my medical records. I told him that I did not know. He told me that, based on that earlier diagnosis, he was granting me fifty percent service connected disability. That entitled me to free mental health services with the V.A. Mental Health Clinic, as well as compensation. I was thankful.

I used the compensation to move into an assisted living facility. It was a good place to be at the time. I did not have to worry about my basic needs. They fixed my meals. A maid service cleaned the house. I had one roommate. That did not bother me. There was a television to watch. I had my medication. It was in a nice neighborhood near the University of Nebraska Medical Center. I would walk down the sidewalk taking in the scenery. It was relaxing. Later, as a peer support specialist, it gave me some understanding of what my peers experienced living in a group home. Unfortunately for my peers, not all group homes are in nice neighborhoods, so they were unable to stroll around like I was.

While living in the assisted living home, I attended a course on computer applications sponsored by Goodwill. I learned about Microsoft Excel, Access, and Word applications. I picked up on them quick. I also got to practice my keyboarding skills. However, I was not very fast compared to the other students. I was able to get up to 56 words per minute. And, that was on a good day.

During my stay in the V.A. hospital, someone recommended that I contact Community Alliance. It was an organization that specialized in working with individuals who had mental illnesses. So, after I was discharged from the hospital, I went over to see what they could do to help me. They evaluated my needs and assigned me a job coach. He took me over to the Vocational Rehabilitation office where I underwent further testing. It was decided that, because of my attention to detail with the O.C.D., I would make a good computer programmer. It sounded good to me. So, they sent me back to college. This time I attended classes at Metro Community College to earn an Associate Degree in Computer Programming Technology. I was given credit for courses I took in my other degrees. As a result, my studies lasted only about a year and a half.

During that time the owner of the assisted living facility raised the rent. I could no longer afford to live there. I prepared to live on the streets. When my ex-wife and her husband found out, they offered to let me rent a small portion of their basement. They said that they were not going to let the father of our son be turned out on the streets if they had room in their home to put me up. I took them up on their generous offer. I not only had a place to stay, but I got to spend more time with my son.

# I WAS A PEER SUPPORT SPECIALIST

Years later, as a peer support specialist for The Salvation Army, I would sometimes come across a peer who also was living in the basement of some family member or ex-spouse. I was able to empathize with their experience. On occasion the peers I met with were not so fortunate and were forced to live in a shelter. Still, my experience enabled me to connect with them.

While studying at the community college, I met a lady in one of my computer courses that worked for a software company. Through her referral I was able to interview for a programming position. I was hired. The company hired a lot of programmers, as they prepared for the Y2K (year 2000) conversion. I made more than I had ever made before. I took my son on a vacation to the Black Hills of South Dakota to see Mount Rushmore. We had a great time. I moved into my own apartment. I lived there nine years.

My good fortune lasted only three years. The Y2K concern passed without incident when the calendar rolled over to the year 2000. Now there were far more programmers than what was needed for the operation of the company. So, five hundred of us were laid off. Other companies did the same. The labour force was flooded with programmers. I was unsuccessful in securing another programming job. I soon learned that employers had their pick of programmers. One had to have seven years hands on experience just to be considered for a position. I had only three years of experience. I was out of luck.

I needed to pay my bills, so I went to work for a temp agency. They sent me out to an insurance company where I spent my time stapling policies together. Then someone else entered the data into their computer system. After that someone filed the paper policies. I made $8.00 dollars an hour. I had to get creative with my budget, but I was able to pay my bills. I moved into a smaller apartment within the same complex, so I did not get penalized for breaking the original lease.

The real stress in the position was that I did not know from one day to the next if I had a job. In the mean time I looked for a more permanent position. Without much luck, I might add. I was very frustrated, stressed, and sinking again into a deep dark cold place.

Finally, on the way home, I lost it. Overcome with thoughts of self-harm, I found myself in the V.A. hospital emergency room. The psychiatrist on call recommended that, for my health, I needed to be admitted into the hospital. The problem was that there were no beds available in Omaha. As a result, I was taken over a hundred miles by ambulance to a V.A. hospital in Iowa. I was met at the door by a staff member and escorted to a room and put to bed.

I stayed in the hospital for ten days. They wanted to keep me for thirty days. I was doing pretty good. But, as it got closer to the first of the following month, I once again started to increase in anxiety. I needed to raise the money to pay my rent. I did not know what to do.

John Friday

I convinced the hospital staff to let me go. They put me on a bus back to Omaha. Once I returned home, I did not know where else to turn but my church. I told them that if they helped me with rent, I would pay them back as soon as possible. The St. Vincent de Paul Society paid my rent for the month. It was a one-time deal.

I went back to the temp agency seeking work. This time they assigned me to a temporary software technical support position. I was on the telephone helping customers install newly purchased software on their computers. I got paid $10.00 an hour. I was feeling a lot more confident, even if it was a temporary seasonal position.

I got a phone call from an old programming friend, informing me that one of our managers, who had been laid off with us, was looking to hire people as high-speed laser printer operators. He had been hired by a data company to set up a print room to process their clients' data into paper products.

I interviewed for one of the position slots and was hired. I picked up on the job tasks quickly. My trainer liked my work ethic, and the speed with which I took to the job. She took me under her wing, and soon had me training other new hires on the printers while she trained some on other types of printers. I took to it like a fish takes to water. I liked what I did and stayed with the company for five years.

Over the course of my time as a printer operator, I continued to receive services from the V.A. Mental Health Clinic. Mostly it was just periodic medication checks. I was on a maintenance dose of my medications.

My job coach from Community Alliance had not given up on me. He felt that there had to be a position that made better use of my skills and experience. In my fourth year as a printer operator he began to talk to me about a career change to what was called a peer support specialist. He felt that I would be good at it. I had not the faintest idea of what he was talking about. He was not able to explain it to me. Instead, he urged me to take the two-week peer support specialist training that Community Alliance offered. The problem was that I could only take off work for a week's vacation at a time. I was stuck.

In my fifth year I was trained to process data provided by the data company's clients and upload it to the mainframe computer. The data came to us on tapes, cartridges, DVDs, and CDs. I had to reformat it using specialized applications. However, there was a deadline from the time I received the data to the time I had to have it uploaded to the mainframe. I was not good at speedy turnover. I started experiencing trouble with my memory. There were moments when I struggled to remember what was supposed to come next. There were different requirements for the processing steps of different data.

I brought the issue up to my psychiatrist. He had my memory evaluated by a specialist. There was no dementia. He determined that it was probably a result of the stress I was experiencing. So, to manage the stress, he prescribed a new medication. Then he went on vacation.

After I started taking the new medication, I blacked out for a week. People later told me that they found it very scary to see. But, they would not tell me what I did. My ex-wife and her husband stepped in to help me. I had been driving around downtown and got lost in an insurance company's parking lot. They came and got me. They took me to the V.A. hospital emergency room. Evidently one of the side effects was a loss of balance. When the doctor heard that I was falling, instead of looking at my medical record to see if I had a recent change in medication, he gave me a walker.

Frustrated with the lack of adequate help, my ex-wife and her husband took me home and put me to bed. They took my supply of medications, and my car. When the medication finally worked its way out of my system, and I woke up, I saw a large sign on the inside of my apartment door. It said "STOP! Your car is not here. Call us when you get up." So, I called them. As I said, they would not tell me very much about what happened. They gave me back my car. From what I understand, after my psychiatrist returned and heard what happened with the emergency room staff and the walker, he had a thing or two to say to them.

When I returned to work, my manager and co-workers would not talk about it. However, I had been taken off my position of uploading data to the mainframe and reassigned to the mailroom. I weighed packages and put shipping labels on them. Then I made certain that the mail made the deadline for being picked up by the various shipping carriers, like UPS, FedEx, etc. It was not long before my supervisor was admonishing me to speed up.

Then my job coach told me about an opening for a part-time peer support specialist with The Salvation Army. He felt that it was the perfect position for me, given my mental health experiences. I judged that, if I made $10.00 an hour, with my V.A. disability compensation check, I would be able to pay my bills. So, as I noted before, I applied for the position and was hired. Then my recovery journey really kicked into gear.

God is gracious.

* * *

# 9 THE V.A. FACTOR

*God is gracious.*

      Over the years that I have used the V.A. Mental Health Clinic services I have had several psychiatrists. I had a nurse practitioner for a while. Then she referred me to a psychiatrist again. She said that she felt that she could not do me justice. One of my diagnoses is borderline personality disorder. I have been told that it is a difficult diagnosis to treat. One should try it from my end.

      I also had a therapist who practiced cognitive behavioral therapy (CBT). Cognitive behavioral therapy addresses issues of how a person thinks. My understanding is that the way a person thinks influences their behaviors. It is effective for people who struggle with major depression. So, they say. I could be wrong.

      I would see my therapist periodically. I remember one occasion where I was feeling down about my military service. I felt bad because I believed that I had not done enough in service to my country, as compared to the sacrifices of other troops. I enlisted in the Air Force because I did not want to get killed in some rice paddy in South Vietnam. I was no hero.

      My therapist was a veteran, too. The way my therapist explained it to me, I had made a commitment to serve in the Air Force, giving myself over to the powers that be. I was willing to go wherever they wanted to use me. I had volunteered a lot to serve overseas, including South Vietnam. The military sent me where they needed me, sometimes on classified missions. I served in the Philippines, Thailand and a few other places. Violent crime was the big issue while I was there, though.

      My therapist pointed out that I had served with honor and deserved to be recognized as a veteran. By putting myself down I was dishonoring other veterans who also made the commitment to serve in whatever way our country saw fit. That made me think. I guess I except that I also served my country with honor in whatever way they deemed fit. I know the others did. And, I do not mean to dishonor anyone. I guess that was an example of CBT changing the way I felt about myself. CBT did benefit me.

As for the therapist, on one occasion I was having difficulty with intrusive thoughts that were very scary. It was not an unusual experience with my obsessive-compulsive disorder. Steven King has nothing over my thoughts. What typically bothers me about these thoughts is the danger of having strong urges to act upon those thoughts.

I had been becoming agitated whenever I was around young men, like in the grocery store. I was experiencing feelings of aggression toward them, and I did not know why. Because of those thoughts and urges, when my therapist referred to them as "just" thoughts, I became very upset with him. They were not "just" thoughts to me. They were very powerful. I wanted to drop him as my therapist. In my mind, he had no idea of the threat my thoughts sometimes posed and what that was like. I explained that to my nurse practitioner, but she directed me to talk it out with him first. When I shared with him how I took what he said, he apologized. So, I stayed with him.

I was working as a peer support specialist at the Friendship Program, Inc. where I met a young lady who was also a veteran. She shared with me her experience of dialectic behavioral therapy (DBT). She talked about mindfulness practices and the different DBT skills that she was learning from her counselor. She noted that the V.A. was sending her to this counselor. The DBT was helping her a lot. I decided that was what I wanted in my therapy experience, too.

When I told my therapist that I wanted to switch from CBT to DBT, he said that he was trained in DBT and could help me. He went on to say that I only needed the mindfulness practices, so he was going to focus on that. I gave him the benefit of a doubt.

But in talking with the young lady at Friendship, what she described that she was learning in her DBT studies was not what I was being taught. My therapist explained that mindfulness was a way of looking at the world. It was a discipline. He said that there were no mindfulness skills that one could do. But, that was not the full story, as the young lady described it. The impression I got was that there were DBT skills that could help me weather the mental illness storm.

I contacted the young lady's counselor and arranged to meet with her. After our discussion, the counselor advised me that, if I wanted to work with her, I should go through my nurse practitioner to get authorized to take DBT from her. I approached my nurse practitioner and explained what I wanted. She noted that DBT was not offered through the V.A. Mental Health Clinic. It was offered through a contracted mental health provider. I made my case and was soon seeing my new counselor.

John Friday

As I met with my new counselor I began learning the concept of mindfulness and wise mind. I learned about finding the middle ground between the rational mind and the emotional mind. I learned exercises to help me develop mindfulness practice. She introduced me to some DBT applications on my smart phone that I began to use. Over the coming year I learned various skills: mindfulness, interpersonal effectiveness, emotion regulation, and distress tolerance. I emailed my counselor daily diary cards, evaluating my progress in the skills.

I met with her twice a week. Once was in group, where we were introduced to the DBT skills and discussed them. We met later in the week one-on-one to discuss how I was doing with mindfulness practice and the DBT skills. I invested myself whole heartedly in this pursuit.

January 12th, 2018, I retired from the Friendship Program, Inc. In February I wound up in the hospital for mental health reasons. I had become suicidal in response to an episode of cognitive dissonance. My stay in the hospital lasted a week. During that time, I experienced the importance of eating a balanced meal three times a day. I experienced the benefit of exercising daily. And, one of the groups I attended talked about cognitive dissonance. After the group, I talked to the psychologist that gave the group. I realized that it was just such an experience that led to my break down. It got me to thinking.

After I was released from the hospital I carried on with the DBT skills and started practicing Tai Chi with my wife. She had obtained a DVD of Tai Chi for beginners. It was great.

I started attending group again, as well as meeting twice a week one-on-one with my counselor. I wanted to try and understand a value system that, every time I was overwhelmed with stress, led me to react with urges to self-harm. I wanted to know more about cognitive dissonance. So, we began to explore that in our sessions. I wanted to develop skills that would help me respond differently. I added the DBT skills that I was learning to my WRAP.

Something else came up in my discussions with my counselor, that I took up with my new psychiatrist. We began to question what was behind some of my experiences of projects that I took on. For example, I wrote my first book in only eight weeks. I created power point presentations for four twelve-week Pathways to Recovery modules in a matter of weeks. I painted five watercolor paintings for an art exhibit in just a few weeks. On each occasion I was energized and stayed up working for a few days on the weekends. I would stay up late on work nights. My wife said that I pushed myself. I could not see it.

The question was "Were these episodes of mania?" There were definite crashes of depression that followed. My diagnosis of major depression was adjusted to bipolar 2. I began to research that diagnosis in the DSM-5.

# I WAS A PEER SUPPORT SPECIALIST

There were times when I had grandiose ideas like selling print copies of my artwork online on a personal website. I started a business called JFriday's Studio. Nothing became of it. No one bought any prints. It was not long before I closed that business.

Later, I got the bright idea to start a peer support business called Omaha Peer Support Services. As a peer support specialist, peers had asked me if there was a way to pursue peer support without joining an agency's program. The peers did not want to attend any other activities required by the agency. They said that they just wanted access to peer support services. I could not find anyone that just offered peer support. So, I started this business. But, in the long run that did not pan out, either. I was going to charge $15.00 an hour. However, the peers that needed the peer support were not able to pay that amount.

There were a couple of organizations, however, that contracted me to facilitate courses of Pathways to Recovery, like I did for the Friendship Program. One group fell apart before we saw the fourth module. The other group did very well. Discussions were very interesting. I was happy for them. However, it was a one-time contract. Seeing that this was going nowhere, I closed this business, too.

CBT and DBT each impacted the peer support services I gave. As we saw above, CBT influenced my self-image. DBT was developed to work with individuals who had borderline personality disorder, like myself. It provided the skills that helped me in my relationships with others. It addresses my perceptions of the world, how I communicate with others, how I cope with my thoughts and feelings, and more. My experience of these therapies became a part of my journey's story of the mental health system that I shared at times with others. It became the source experiences that enabled us to empathize with each other and to realize that we were not alone in these struggles.

Facilitating the groups of Pathways to Recovery helped me to understand the recovery journey better. I listened to other peers' perspectives and experiences of their recovery journeys. That helped me, even as I reflected on my own worldview. It was as much a journey of self-discovery for me, as it was for the participants in my groups. Through our sharing of ourselves, I came to better understand intentional peer support's fourth task, "moving toward". I grew to realize that, in our own unique ways, peer support nurtures each of us through our peer-to-peer relationships toward the fullness of our recovery journey, the actualization of our life goals, a life that thrives in its fullest potential.

WRAP has no less impacted my recovery journey, enabling me to recover my wellness when I find myself in the depth of my struggles with the storms of mental illness. Through the WRAP groups I have facilitated, as well as in our peer-to-peer relationships, I have learned from the witness of peers' experiences with proven wellness tools that they found helpful to managing their struggles with their mental illnesses.  In turn, what I have learned about taking care of myself has become a part of the worldview I bring to my peer support relationships.

One wellness tool that was suggested to me that has worked very well for me is taking a drive in the country.  My wife and I will sometimes just get in the car and head out for the wide-open spaces.  There is no set destination; we just drive.  Most of the time we do not play the radio or engage in any conversation.  We just take in the peaceful sights of the farmland and the low rolling hills.  On one occasion we started out in Omaha, NE and did not turn back until we had entered South Dakota.  We even drove through a native American reservation.  It was so relaxing.

Another wellness tool that I use is sitting out on our deck overlooking the backyard.  It too is peaceful.  We have a very quiet neighborhood.  During warm weather I sit out there and watch the squirrels chase each other or eat the peanuts my wife puts out for them.  She is a real animal activist.  Sometimes she will come out on the deck and join me.  We have three cats and they will roam the backyard.  One cat, Samantha, likes to stalk the birds that also drop in for bread and peanuts.  She never has been able to catch one.  But, she does not let that discourage her.  These are but a few of the wellness tools I like to use.

My peer support services have grown and evolved as I have grown in so many ways.  My recovery journey, my experiences of my mental illnesses, my experiences of the mental healthcare system, my experiences of WRAP and the Pathways to Recovery groups, my experiences of my peer-to-peer relationships, and so much more have all impacted the peer support specialist I became.  Peer support changed my life.  I will never be the same.

God is gracious.

※ ※ ※

# 10 MY MENTAL HEALTH

---
*God is gracious.*

---

  I went to see my DBT counselor today. Our conversation got me to thinking about my disorders. The one that is most on my mind and that we talked about the most is the borderline personality disorder. As many doctors say, it is the most difficult to treat. Yet, it is the disorder that dialectic behavioral therapy (DBT) was created to address. It is not even considered to be my main disorder, but it complicates things.
  My wife has noted on one occasion that my behavior makes her think that I sometimes act like a jerk. I wonder what she and others see that I do not see. Even my counselor acknowledges that I do not see it. She goes on to say that is part of the problem with borderline personality disorder. Everything seems okay to me. I have difficulty with attachments. Yet, sometimes I have intense feelings of irritability, anxiety, and even anger.
  My counselor says that typically women with borderline personality disorder often have issues with feelings of abandonment. I have not had feelings of abandonment since I was fourteen, when my mom dumped me in a home for boys and I cried myself to sleep. I cannot think of a time since then that I have shed a tear. I lack attachments. I do not feel the same things in relationships that people without a personality disorder feel. Just about all my adult life women have been objects with whom I medicated myself. Echoing what my ex-wife had complained about in the past, my current wife has also noted that sometimes she feels that we seem more like roommates than husband and wife. As my counselor observed, I have difficulty understanding that. I do not see things from their point of view, like attachments.
  The question comes up as to why I do not form attachments. My counselor thinks that it goes back to those early days when attachments were supposed to be formed. My mother and I always argued. I got the feeling that I was an object used to meet her need, especially financially. When I was twelve years old, she tried to

find me a job to help support the family. And, when I did get work, I gave all I earned to her. When I first enlisted in the Air Force, she cried because I would not buy her a house. I tried to explain to her that she was not my wife. The government did not pay me for supporting my mother.

At times I felt that my mother was incestuous. Talks with her sometimes made me feel dirty. She did not respect any boundaries. At times, she even tried to tell me about her and my father's sex life. She described him as a monster. I had to scream at her to get her to stop. I withdrew from her.

After the divorce, my family self-destruct. My father long since withdrew from me. He was not the only one. There was little or no contact from my grandmother, aunts, uncles, and cousins. There was nothing to fill the void.

In high school, I kept to myself. I was afraid of the other teenagers. Yet, the teenagers I had contact with seemed to like me. Or, at least they liked the artwork I did. With my art teacher's permission, I used to take lunch in the art room and draw. I do not remember if I even ate lunch. I spent my time in school drawing or sleeping in class. I felt no attachments there. I never went on a date or had a relationship, let alone with another teenager. As for my maternal grandfather, after helping me get a job to help support myself, he pretty much left me to my own resources. I think that I loved him. He was always kind to me. But, I do not feel that I had an attachment to him, either.

As a young adult in the Air Force, I pretty much kept to myself there, too. Except, that is, unless I was working on an aircraft with someone. That might be when I was refuelling an aircraft. Even when aircraft specialists were on the plane I was off by myself, taking care of some other maintenance chore. When I was off duty, even when I was in a crowd, like in the airman's club, I was alone. I did not hang out with people that much. There was martial arts, and then there was SCUBA diving. I travelled with the aircraft.

There were no relationships of attachments. I laid bar girls, but I did not date; not even when I was stationed in the United States. After I got alcohol poisoning from over indulging in hard liquor, I quit bar hopping. One guy who used to follow me around like a puppy in the Philippines, quit calling me friend when I would not go out drinking with him and his buddies in Thailand. There just were not any attachments. That was just the way it was. I was never lonely, though. And, I guess that is strange. I suppose that is the borderline personality disorder. But, I do not understand it.

Sometimes, even today, there are mood swings. I get frustrated at being asked to do something I do not know how to do. I start getting irritable, angry, and volatile. When I feel pressured to do it anyway, I have been known to explode in a rage. I have learned, since becoming a peer support specialist, to practice deep breathing exercises and clench my fists to de-escalate the anger I feel. My counselor said that some of the DBT skills are for learning how to relate to and interact with people in ways that they understand. My counselor went on to compare it to the old saying "fake it till you make it."

My counselor said that it is apparent to her that my wife does not have a personality disorder. That makes her a good model from whom I can learn how to interact with people. My counselor said that it will take time. I am sixty-six years old. It is feasible that I might go the rest of my life without learning. That is just the way it is. Thing is, that notion does not bother me.

Perhaps it is because of the borderline personality disorder that I am not triggered by the sharing peers do with me. When peers share some of their story, I can share some of my story that relates to it. But, it does not get me down. If anything, it is nice to know that we are not alone in our struggles with mental illness. I empathize rationally, rather than from the heart. So, I do not appear so cold.

I find the borderline personality disorder interesting. But, that is probably because I have it. Recently, I ended up in the hospital because of severe suicidal urges. That was a reaction I had to an incident of cognitive dissonance, being caught in the middle of a conflict between other individuals.

Couple the borderline personality disorder with depression, and things get complicated. Most of the time I have avoided suicide, even though I have had strong suicidal thoughts. I have avoided it because of two things: I did not want to go to Hell, and I did not want to hurt my son through the way I died.

However, my feelings of self-harm were different in 1996. Over a period of months, I sank into despair and emotional anguish. As a teacher, I could not get a handle on discipline with a seventh-grade class. I had a good relationship with the sixth-graders. And, the same was true with the eighth-graders. But, I could not get the seventh-graders to behave long enough to teach them anything. And, I did not feel that I had the support of the Principal. Then the parents of one of the seventh-graders yelled at me so loud that the students in the hall could hear. If I fought back, I would not only have lost my job, I probably would have ended up in jail. I wanted to pound the father to a pulp. I felt unappreciated, unsupported, a lack of recognition of my efforts on behalf of the students and a lack of respect. So, I resigned my teaching position.

Unlike other times when I had thoughts of self-harm, my way of thinking changed. The things that seemed crazy to other people made sense to me. Sinking into a deep dark cold abyss of despair and hopelessness, there was no redemption. I concluded that I was made for Hell. I felt that, having my ex-wife tell my son that I had been killed in an automobile accident would protect him from the reality of my own self-destruction. I became resolved to my own demise. The Hell I was condemning myself to seemed less painful than the hell I was experiencing in this life. So, I surmised that, even in Hell, I would find peace. I was resolved to living an act of blasphemy. The only thing I still needed was the sleeping pills. But, the police arrived before I could get the pills. In addition, I could not convince them to let me follow through with the act of liberating myself from this life. I was content to leave this life. The irony was that people started appearing in my life, passing me from one person to another. Each one met my need in some way, until I was redeemed and could once again care for myself.

And notwithstanding the borderline personality disorder, even with the lack of attachment, I think that I care. I am not sure in what way the disorder manifests itself. I am still learning. I love my wife and care about her. I have been there for her when she has suffered a great loss. And, I consoled her.

As a peer support specialist, I feel fulfilled when I can be there with a person and share in their recovery journey and strengthen our peer-to-peer relationship within the limitations and confines of mental illness. I am still growing and still learning about my mental illnesses, especially the borderline personality disorder.

I understand the obsessive-compulsive disorder a little better. It is an anxiety disorder. I feel the anxiety when certain things happen, and, as a result, I respond with compulsive behaviors to relieve the anxiety. Sometimes I feel anxious because of the feeling of contamination. When it happens, I am compelled to wash my hands to remove the contamination. At other times, to avoid contamination, I will use a paper towel or the sleeve of my sweater to open a door. Other times it might be an overwhelming sense of doubt. I feel compelled to check and recheck something I did, like locking a door. Or, it might be the fear that I made a mistake. So, I will recheck the quality of my work numerous times. It is what made it so difficult for me to keep up with the tasks on a production line. I never got the job done. In some situations, I hoarded things, like books. They were all good references, and I told myself that someday I would read them. The problem was that I never had the time to do so.

Depression is the hurricane of the storms of my mental illnesses. I crash into a dark place without the energy to resist. The winds of the storm blow me about. The rains weigh me down. But, since becoming a peer support specialist, I have learned strategies that help me weather the storm of symptoms and survive until a brighter day comes. And, brighter days do come. There are times when I enjoy life. I can and do experience happiness. I can and do thrive.

I accept the fact that science indicates at times there is a chemical imbalance in my brain. And, I accept that it somehow effects the way I feel and think and behave. But, I am no longer at its mercy. I can cope and manage the symptoms. So, my life is not a tragedy. It is full of possibilities and adventures. I am never bored.

# I WAS A PEER SUPPORT SPECIALIST

Mania is something else that I am learning more about. Do I muster the energy to perform the projects that I envision? Or, do I envision projects on which to focus my energy? It is a question of which comes first, the chicken or the egg. I think that I have the energy first, and then channel it in a creative way. I find an object to act upon creatively, like an art project such as watercolor painting. Even my power point presentations are subjects of creative expression. My writing of books is, too. When we were expecting the birth of our son, I decorated a nursery for him. As a teacher, my research of students' academic records became the basis of custom lesson plans for each child's learning. That, too, was an object of creative expression. The remedial reading course that I developed was an object of creative expression. The library I put together for Safe Harbor Peer Services was an object of creative expression. I always had sources of great energy and drive that fed those creative projects. So, were those spurts of energy mania? I do not know.

As I explore the mental illnesses that I have, I learn more about myself and how these mental illnesses interact and how I can manage their symptoms. I seek to learn the part they play in the adventure of my recovery journey and in the peer support that I provide the peers I serve.

I was a peer support specialist.

And I always will be.

God is gracious.

* * *

# 11 ADDITIONAL SUPPORTS

*God is gracious.*

I have been asked to address those who do not have mental illnesses and/or substance abuse. But, I am not sure of what to say.

My brother suggested that I speak about my involvement with police officers. As a person who has repeatedly been in a mental health state that has required intervention, I want to note that the police officer has been a lifesaver for me. I have noted earlier that in 1996 I had my first encounter with the police stepping in to rescue me from my own self-destructive behavior. They have my undying gratitude and respect.

I imagine that it is an experience that is different than what one is usually involved. Those with mental illnesses are not normally a criminal element of our society. Many see us as broken. And, I am sorry to say that some see us as a threat. However, we are more often a threat to ourselves than others. Although, I must admit that I have been a threat to others on rare occasions. It is not something that I am proud of doing. It is not something that is my typical behavior. It is a time when I needed you most. And, I thank God for you.

In the past, I have been invited to participate in the training of police officers who have volunteered to take the specialized training of the Crisis Intervention Team (C.I.T.). I was honored. And, I made certain to thank the officers for their service. I feel that I am indebted to you all.

Earlier I described how the officer in 1996 stepped into my life and saw to it that I received the professional medical help that I needed. But, that was not the only time. There was an incident a few months later when I contemplated suicide by cop.

I was on the phone with a person from Catholic Charities trying to arrange an appointment with a therapist. The person with whom I was speaking asked me about the kinds of thoughts that I was having. But, I was having racing thoughts about ways to self-harm. The one I picked to share with her was the thought I was having about acquiring an unloaded handgun and pointing it at a police officer. Then the officer would have to fire his or her weapon, killing me: suicide by cop.

About the time I shared that thought, there was a knock at my apartment door. I answered it and standing there in the doorway was a group of police officers. The officer in charge was concerned and not happy with my plan. He said that he had been listening to my conversation through the door.

He shared his feelings about my plan. He noted that it was a terrible thing to do to a person, especially to a police officer. He asked how I thought he would feel to have shot me only to find out later that my gun was empty; that I had used him for completing suicide. I had selfishly not considered how the police officer would feel.

I was concerned with the problem of a person with a mental illness passing the required checks needed before one could purchase a handgun. From what I have seen on television, I have come to realize that a realistic looking toy gun could serve the purpose just as well.

I was impressed with the officer's sincere compassion for my wellbeing. Like the officer in 1996, he talked me through the process of being handcuffed and taken to the squad car. My attention was on him. It never crossed my mind that the neighbors might gossip about what they witnessed that day, as I was driven off to the hospital. I am sure that it would have only added to the stigma of mental illness. And, that is a shame.

I have one bit of advice regarding the way I was transported. The officer sat me in the front seat of his cruiser. Between he and me was a shotgun. The whole time I was riding to the hospital I kept thinking of putting my mouth over the barrel and blowing off my head. I just could not figure out how to pull the trigger with handcuffs on. Good thing.

At the C.I.T. training, I have participated in different ways. The first time I helped I was teamed up with a police officer who was an instructor. We observed scenarios where the trainees were paired together and responding to a mental health crisis call. For the most part they did very well. During our debriefing of their performance I made a few suggestions regarding things they did that I felt would have escalated the crisis. For the most part, though, they did very well.

The next year I was invited to share my story with the officers at the C.I.T. training. I sat on a panel of peers in front of the officers. I described my mental illness journey. And, I thanked them for their service.

The year after that I was invited to co-present a discussion of the Crisis Plan portion of the Wellness Recovery Action Plan (WRAP). The power point presentation explained what the parts of the plan are, and how it can be used to help the peer in a mental health crisis. We also passed around a couple of WRAP workbooks, so the police officers knew what to look for. The presentation was appreciated. I enjoyed my part of the presentation and felt that I had helped.

On one occasion months later, a police officer brought a peer to Safe Harbor Peer Services center to spend some time with a peer support specialist. The officer noted that he remembered me from the C.I.T. training. I thanked him and greeted the peer into the center. The police officer returned to his duty. I was gratified that the officer remembered me from the training.

I guess the thing I want to tell police officers is to trust your training. I know that there are some people with mental health issues who dread being placed in handcuffs, particularly in front of their family and neighbors. I am not one of them. I understand that it is for the safety of all involved in the crisis intervention. I would ask that, as have other officers, you simply talk me through the process, reassuring me that everything is going to be okay. Be compassionate. I am a person, too. In the moment you see me, I am most likely not myself. God bless you.

My counselor asked me to speak to the family. I note that there are peer support specialists trained to provide peer support to the family. To be designated a family peer support specialist, one must have a family member who has a mental illness and/or substance abuse issues. The family peer support specialist may also have mental illness and/or substance abuse issues themselves, but that is not a requirement. Because of their firsthand experience with their family member, they share in the challenges and concerns for that loved one's wellbeing.

But, before I talked about the family members of the peer, I wanted you to know that there is peer support out there for you, too. And, I wanted you to know that you too could be a peer support specialist, providing support to the family members of others.

As the family of a loved one with mental health issues, you are a very important part of their life and play no less an important role in their life than any mental health provider. As a family member with special issues, I need your support. It is important to me that you validate my experience of mental illness. That can be difficult for you to do, but it is very important to do. We know that it can be very painful at times for you to face our mental health condition, let alone understand it.

My brother has had to take difficult stands at times. He had to be patient with me and support my doctor's decision to hospitalize me, even as I was screaming over the phone at him to get me the hell out of there. It was not one of my better days, but my brother took a position that supported me even when I could not see it. He reassured me that I was getting the help that I needed, and that he loved me. He is my hero.

My ex-wife and her husband have stepped up to the plate on more than one occasion to support me in my time of crisis. Their actions saved my life. The same is true for my pastor. So, even the community has a role in providing support to those with mental illnesses, especially when in a crisis. And, I thank all of you.

But, you have a role in my life even when there is not a crisis. Your love and patience and support are so desperately needed in my recovery journey as I work toward a life that actualizes my fullest potential. It means so very much for you to be there for me. I am thinking of my present wife as well as my brother.

My wife supports me in times when I need support in coping with the storms of my mental illness. We sit out on the deck, absorbing the quiet and peace of the backyard while feeding the squirrels peanuts. Or, we go for a drive in the country, sharing the experience of the tranquil farmland scenery. We take a break and share time together, just being together. She listens without judgment as I share some of my story and challenges of the day. She gives me hugs for no other reason than she loves me. She is patient with me and accepting, especially when she is unable to understand why I am the way I am in my mental illness. She, too, has stood by me as I sought help in the V.A. hospital emergency room. She has been encouraging in my efforts to learn more effective ways to manage my symptoms as I have attended outpatient therapy. Thank you, my love, for all you do for me. I hope to be there for you, too.

There is also a trained peer support specialist for the youth. The specialist does not have to be a youth. However, they must have started experiencing the symptoms of their mental illness while in their youth. That way they can empathized and validate youth who are currently experiencing the onset of the symptoms of mental illness. That helps the youth accept that they are not alone. There is a peer who has walked in their shoes. The peer is not only a role model of one on their recovery journey but is also a beacon of hope for a bright future.

God is gracious.

* * *

John Friday

## 12 ARTWORK AND MY MENTAL ILLNESS

---
*God is gracious.*

---

Throughout my life I have tinkered with art, mostly focusing on the technical skills used with various art media, rather than as an expression of my 'self'. Much of what I learned came from reading books on art media, as well as experimenting with that media. In college I took courses in basic drawing, art history, and philosophy of art.

One day in 2012, a peer support specialist co-worker shared her art journal with me. She described how it told her recovery journey story. I realized that my skill with art was an opportunity for me to share my own life journey with mental illness and trauma. Since then I have produced a variety of watercolor paintings expressing that part of myself that is a survivor of multiple traumas and of struggles with mental illness. I had found my 'story'.

In 2015 and 2017, as a peer support specialist, I have shared my artwork with the residents of the Lincoln Regional Center in Lincoln, Nebraska. I put together power point presentations of my work each time. The Lincoln Regional Center is an institution where individuals with severe mental illness issues are confined. The residents said that they appreciated my sharing my artwork with them.

Over a three-year period, beginning in 2014, I have donated four of the paintings to the Friendship Program, Inc., a mental health rehabilitation center. They were part of a fundraising raffle during their open house festivities. It was very successful. And, it was a pleasure to participate.

God is gracious.

**Chaos**

This abstract watercolor painting is reflective of a lot of the emotional storm of my life. The written words in the picture add to the cognitive confusion of the storm.

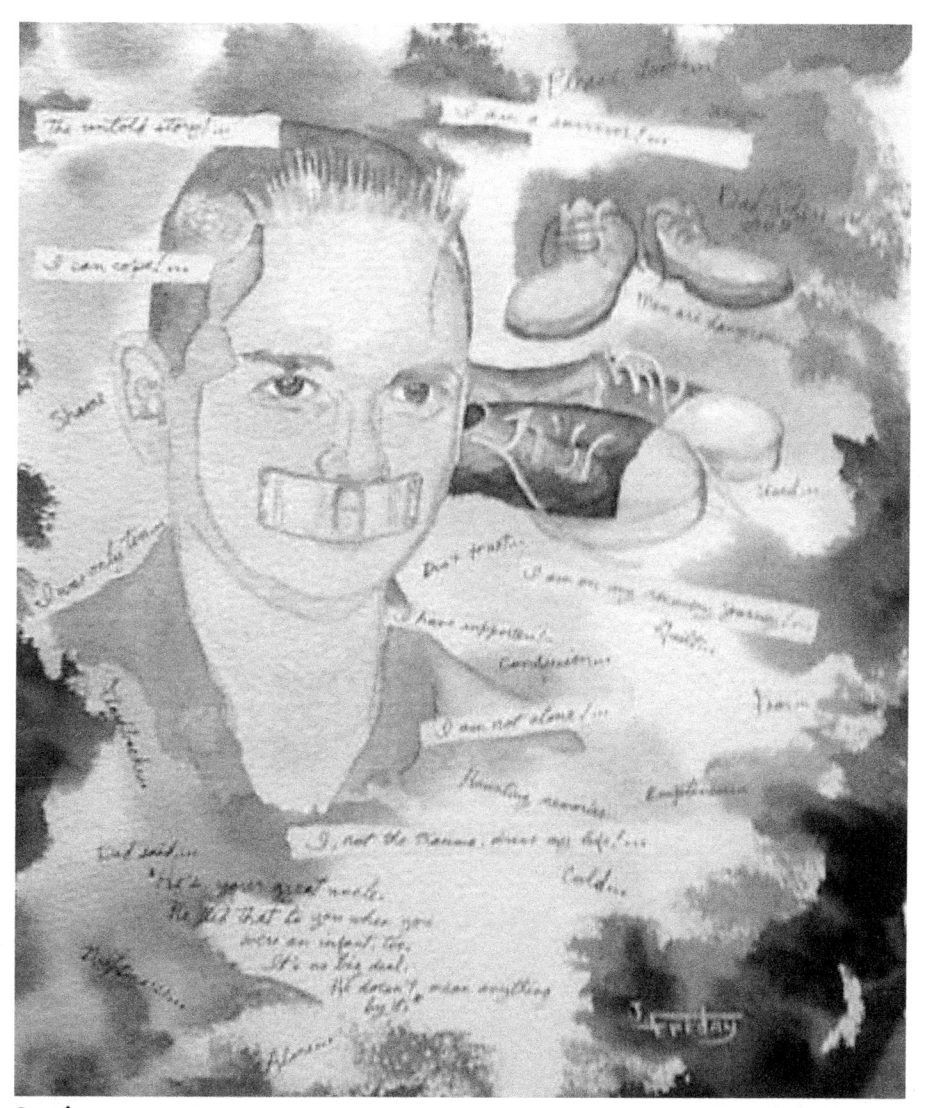

**Survivor**

Survivor" is a work that explores my feelings 'then' (the tragic encounter I had as a child with a great uncle that no child should ever have), and my thoughts and feelings 'now' many decades later.

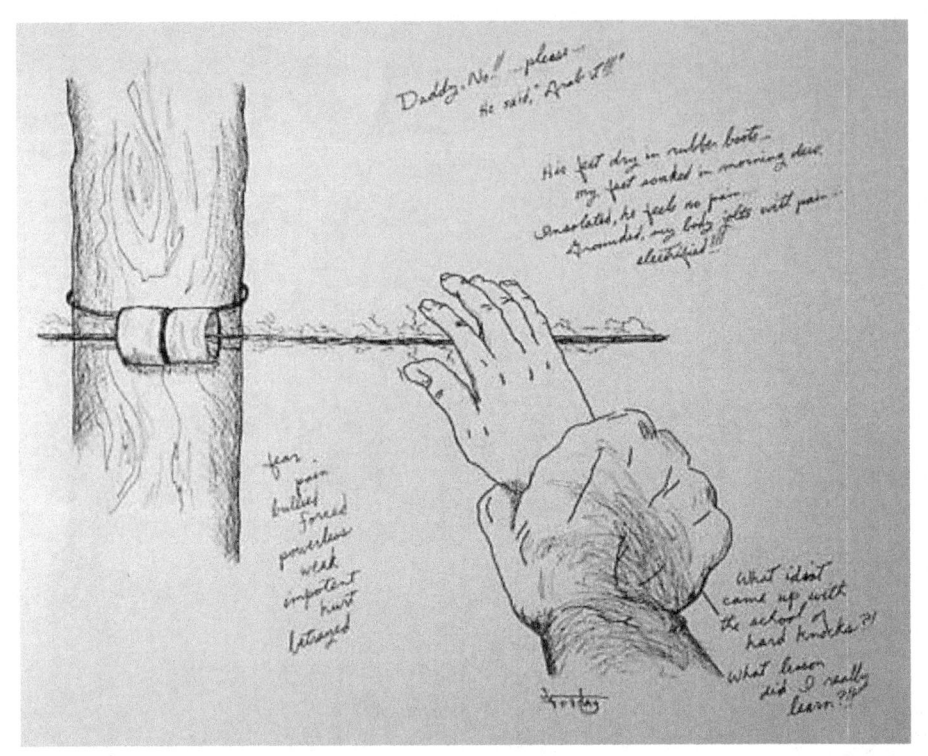

**Betrayed**

"Betrayed" is an exploration of my 'self', with roots in my childhood experiences, particularly my relationship with my dad. This picture portrays the time that my father electrocuted me.

**The Birth of Faith**

This painting portrays a time in my twenties when God touched my heart and started to draw me closer to Himself.

# John Friday

**Heart and Soul**

### *Heart and Soul*

"God's Love for us...for me.
    It is always personal.

Just think of how He is greater than the Universe.
    He spans it and permeates it.

In His immense being He is pure Love.
    Yet, in that huge infinite being He knows me
    in my smallness...   by name
        and Loves me.

And in that smallness and weakness,
    My sinfulness is never and can never be
        greater than His Love for me.

Oh, how my heart burns with my Love for Him...
    My Lord...
        My God!!!"

By John Friday

John Friday

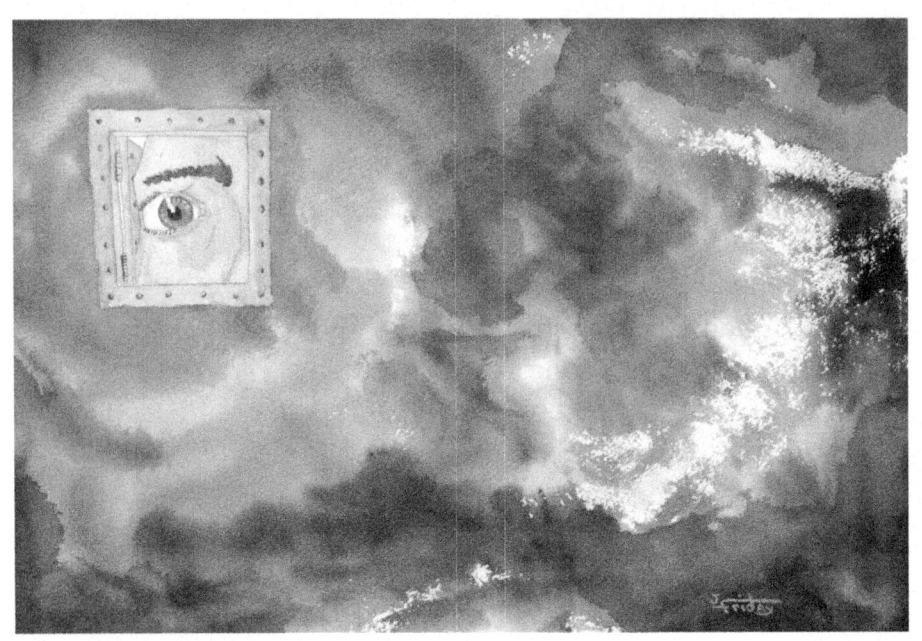

**A Glimpse into My Soul**

This watercolor painting portrays a time in my mental health journey when mental health providers tried to examine my psychological 'self'.

**Without Hope**

This painting is an expression of my feelings of hopelessness that I experienced in my own self-destructive state of mind in 1996.

**Daddy's Little Clown**

This work reflects my own resentment of my father using me as an object for his own sense of humor and exploitation. Looking under the smile of the clown's mask, one sees an expression of despair on the little boy's face.

**Sidewalk Tenant**

Carl gave me permission to do a painting of him. He lived on the streets of Omaha, Nebraska. On occasion I would bring out lunch for the both of us and we would share a meal. He died in 2017.

**Monk in Galilee**

This is a watercolor composition of a monk sitting in a field of flowers in Galilee. For me, he is pondering his relationship as a part of Creation with his Creator.

**Sea of Galilee**

This painting is simply a rendition of a sunrise on the Sea of Galilee. It is the dawn of a new day in the Holy Land. Creation is waking.

John Friday

# BIBLIOGRAPHY AND RECOMMENDED READINGS

American Psychiatric Association. (2013). *Diagnostic and Statistical Manual of Mental Disorders.* 5$^{th}$ Ed. Arlington, VA: American Psychiatric Association.

Capacchione, Lucia. Ph.D. (2002). *The Creative Journal: The Art of Finding Yourself.* 2$^{nd}$ Ed. Franklin Lakes, NJ: New Page Books.

Chamberlin, Judi. (1978). *On Our Own: Patient-Controlled Alternatives to the Mental Health System.* New York: McGraw-Hill Book Company.

Copeland, Mary Ellen. Ph.D. *WRAP is...*
www.mentalhealthrecovery.com/wrap-is

Copeland, Mary Ellen. Ph.D. (1997). *Wellness Recovery Action Plan.* Dummerston, Vermont: Peach Press.
www.wrapandrecoverybooks.com/store

Copeland, Mary Ellen. Ph.D. (2016). *WRAP and Peer Support Handbook: Working Together to Reclaim Our Lives.* Dummerston, Vermont: Peach Press.
www.wrapandrecoverybooks.com/store

Copeland, Mary Ellen. Ph.D. (2014). *Wellness Recovery Action Plan Workbook.* Dummerston, Vermont: Peach Press.
www.wrapandrecoverybooks.com/store

Davidson, Lori; McDiarmid, Diane; Higbee, Jean M. (2006). *Pathways to Recovery: Group Facilitator's Guide.* Lawrence, KS: The University of Kansas School of Social Welfare, Office of Mental Health Research & Training.

Mathieu, Francoise. (2012). *The Compassion Fatigue Workbook: Creative Tools for Transforming Compassion Fatigue and Vicarious Traumatization.* New York: Routledge. Taylor & Francis Group.

Mead, Shery. *Defining Peer Support.*
www.intentionalpeersupport.org/articles

Mead, Shery. *Intentional Peer Support: A Personal Retrospective.*
   www.intentionalpeersupport.org/articles

Mead, Shery. MSW.; Copeland, Mary Ellen. Ph.D. (2000). *What Recovery Means to Us.* New York: Plenum Publishers.

Mead, Shery; MacNeil, Cheryl. *Peer Support: What Makes It Unique?*
   www.intentionalpeersupport.org/articles

Mead, Shery. MSW. (2014). *Intentional Peer Support: An Alternative Approach.* Bristol, Vermont.
   www.intentionalpeersupport.org/store

National Alliance on Mental Illness (NAMI). *Bipolar Disorder.*
   www.nami.org/Learn-More/Mental-Health-Conditions/Bipolar-Disorder

National Alliance on Mental Illness (NAMI). *Borderline Personality Disorder.*
   www.nami.org/Learn-More/Mental-Health-Conditions/Borderline-Personality-Disorder

National Alliance on Mental Illness (NAMI). *Depression.*
   www.nami.org/Learn-More/Mental-Health-Conditions/Depression

National Alliance on Mental Illness (NAMI). *Dual Diagnosis.*
   www.nami.org/Learn-More/Mental-Health-Conditions/Related-Conditions/Dual-Diagnosis

National Alliance on Mental Illness (NAMI). *Family Members and Caregivers.*
   www.nami.org/Find-Support/Family-Members-and-Caregivers

National Alliance on Mental Illness (NAMI). *Obsessive-compulsive Disorder.*
   www.nami.org/Learn-More/Mental-Health-Conditions/Obsessive-compulsive-Disorder

National Alliance on Mental Illness (NAMI). *Psychotherapy.*
   www.nami.org/Learn-More/Treatment/Psychotherapy/

Ridgway, Priscilla; McDiarmid, Diane; Davidson, Lori; Bayes, Julie; Ratzlaff, Sarah. (2002). *Pathways to Recovery: A Strengths Recovery Self-Help Workbook.* Lawrence, KS: University of Kansas School of Social Welfare.

Substance Abuse & Mental Health Services Administration

(SAMHSA). *SAMHSA's Working Definition of Recovery: 10 Guiding Principles of Recovery.*
www.samhsa.gov/recovery

Made in the USA
Columbia, SC
12 September 2018